WORLD WAR I

Quilts

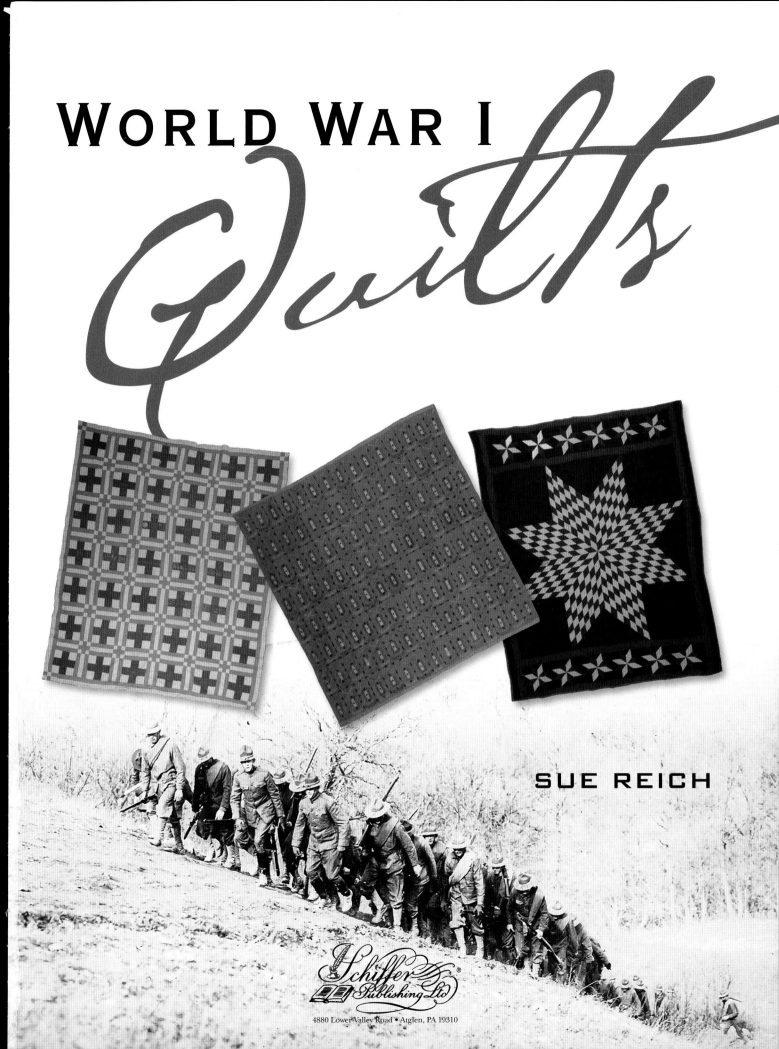

SUE REICH

Schiffer
Publishing Ltd
4880 Lower Valley Road • Atglen, PA 19310

OTHER SCHIFFER BOOKS BY THE AUTHOR

QUILTINGS, FROLICKS & BEES: 100 YEARS OF SIGNATURE QUILTS
978-0-7643-4098-7

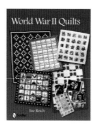

WORLD WAR II QUILTS
978-0-7643-3451-1

QUILTING NEWS OF YESTERYEAR: CRAZY AS A BED QUILT
978-0-7643-2795-7

OTHER SCHIFFER BOOKS ON RELATED SUBJECTS

CIVIL WAR QUILTS
Pam Weeks and Don Beld
978-0-7643-3936-3

QUILTS OF THE OREGON TRAIL
Mary Bywater Cross
978-0-7643-2316-4

UNIFORMS, EQUIPMENT & WEAPONS OF THE AMERICAN EXPEDITIONARY FORCES IN WORLD WAR I
Brett Werner
978-0-7643-2431-4

Copyright © 2014 by Sue Reich
Library of Congress Control Number: 2014950850

Type set in Adobe Caslon Pro & Arial
ISBN: 978-0-7643-4754-2
Printed in China

Published by Schiffer Publishing, Ltd.
4880 Lower Valley Road
Atglen, PA 19310
Phone: (610) 593-1777; Fax: (610) 593-2002
E-mail: Info@schifferbooks.com

For our complete selection of fine books on this and related subjects, please visit our website at www.schifferbooks.com. You may also write for a free catalog.

This book may be purchased from the publisher. Please try your bookstore first.

We are always looking for people to write books on new and related subjects. If you have an idea for a book, please contact us at proposals@schifferbooks.com.

Schiffer Publishing's titles are available at special discounts for bulk purchases for sales promotions or premiums. Special editions, including personalized covers, corporate imprints, and excerpts can be created in large quantities for special needs. For more information, contact the publisher.

DEDICATED TO THE VETERANS OF ALL AMERICAN WARS

We cherish too, the poppy red
That grows on fields where valor led,
It seems to signal to the skies
That blood of heroes never dies,
But lends a luster to the red
Of the flower that blooms above the dead
In Flanders Fields.

—from "We Shall Keep the Faith,"
Moina Michael, 1918

CONTENTS

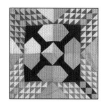

INTRODUCTION

Edward J. Martin USN, Pittsburgh, Pennsylvania, c. 1918

interested in quilting after the Bicentennial. My elderly next-door neighbor, Bertine Southworth, eagerly shared her small collection of family quilts. Bertine was an inveterate story teller. With each of her quilts, there was a tale to be told but none as fascinating as her *Hole in the Barn Door/ Churndash* quilt. The quilt was brought to Ohio from Indiana as an unfinished top by Bertine's mother, Mathilda, for her impending marriage to Vern Southworth, a successful house builder in Bedford. In 1917, Bertine's soon to be brother-in-law, Frank Hoeffler, was shipping off to the battlefront in France: the quilt was quickly tied into a thick comforter for his bed. The wool used

My earliest remembrances of World War I include the poppies handed out to all who attended the Memorial Day and Veterans Day parades near my childhood home in Pittsburgh, and the photo of my grandfather Edward J. Martin in his sailor uniform, set on the mantel of my grandparents' farmhouse in Crawford County, Pennsylvania. Even at a young age, I was instinctively aware of the respect and honor both items commanded. In the 1950s, Memorial Day was usually referred to as Decoration Day and Veterans Day was called Armistice Day.

Fast forward twenty years: just prior to our country's Bicentennial celebration in 1976, my young family settled southeast of Cleveland, Ohio in a town called Bedford. Like many young wives and mothers, I became seriously

"When the Boys Come Home." *The Red Cross Magazine*, March, 1918, page 17.

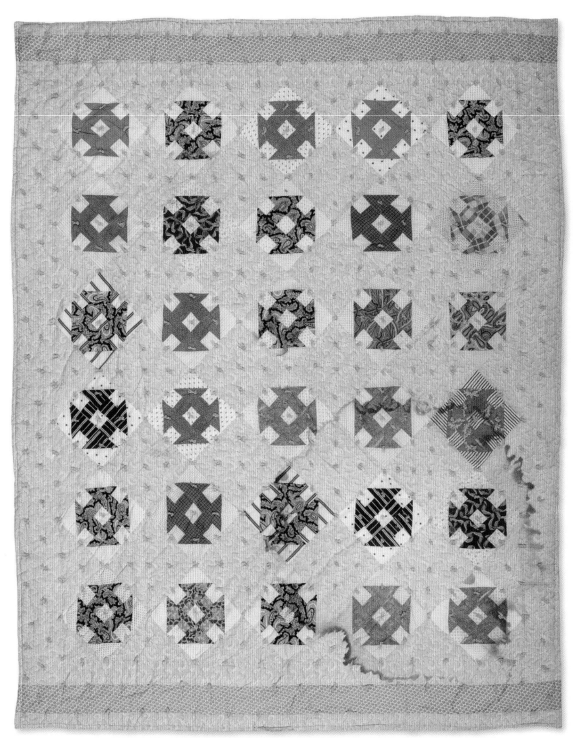

Hole in the Barn Door/Churndash Quilt, c. 1910, hand pieced, hand tied, 66 inches x 82 inches, cotton.

The wool used to tie this quilt was also used to knit socks for the American soldiers in World War I.

1918 Modern Priscilla Knitting instructions for supplies for our soldiers on the battlefront.

Vallee Foulan, France. Stereograph by The Keystone View Company, V18875 "And Now We Lie in Flanders Fields."

to tie the quilt was the same wool that Bertine, her sister Mildred, and her mother used to knit socks and other gear for the American soldiers.

In the late 1990s, I had the opportunity to travel through France, the Low Countries, and Germany. Scattered across the countryside, nestled in grazing and crop fields, are tiny cemeteries with neatly arranged white crosses in small fenced enclosures. They represent stark reminders of the battles of World War 1 fought on that soil a mere 80 years earlier. Battle names of Ypres, Verdun, and the Argonne Forest came to mind. These pastoral landscapes were the scene of a living hell during the "Great War" with its trenches, barbed wire and chemical warfare.

Now, nearly 20 years later, with the 100th anniversary commemorative years of World War I, I have a renewed interest in an in-depth study of quilts made between 1914 and 1918. Both the news articles about wartime quiltmaking and the number of quilts made during the war years are much fewer than those of the World War II years. That said, the quilts of World War I are dear and will tug at your heartstrings. With the 100th anniversary commemoration occurring between 2014 and 2018, expect greater focus on this era of world turmoil and "The Great War."

Today, in our Memorial Day and Veterans Day parades, Honor Guards still lead with our country's colors. Soldiers of the bygone wars don their uniforms to march in step and recite the cadence of their units. Boy Scouts and Girl Scouts carry troop banners. Volunteer firemen wave from their polished ladder trunks and pumpers. High school bands play patriotic music and form on town greens and cemeteries for the reading of the names of local soldiers of America's wars. Veterans of past wars sell poppies, the botanical symbol of World War I. America's families remember and honor the great sacrifice of our country's brave men and women who served in the Armed Forces of the United States.

The photo of our family's World War I sailor is still proudly displayed in my home in Connecticut in hopes of passing on a knowledge and understanding to my children and grandchildren that "freedom is not free" and that brave Americans paid a hefty price for the "grand American way."

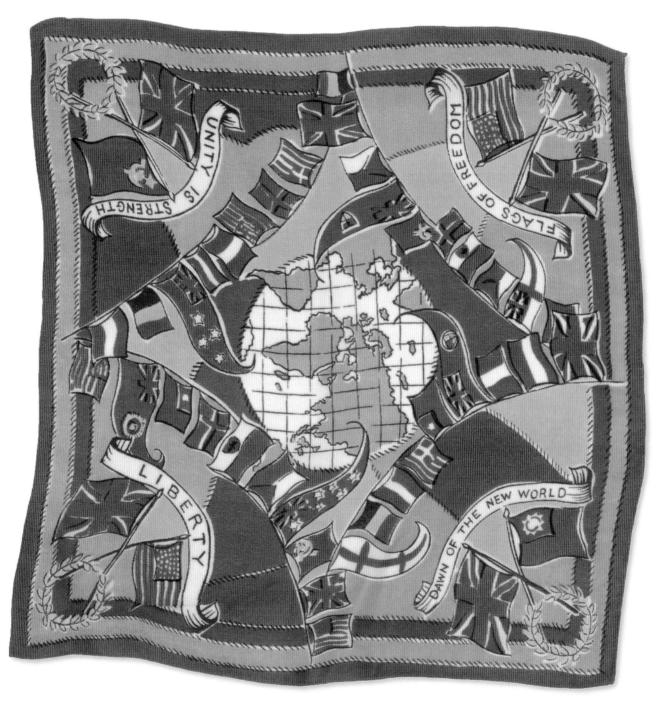

Handkerchief from World War I featuring the flags of our allies.

World War I and World War II Quilt, 60 inches x 80 inches, cotton. This Native American, Honor Roll Quilt was made in 1945 by the W.S.C.S. (Women's Society of Christian Service.) The names of the quiltmakers are inscribed across the top of the quilt. Each diagonal cross is embroidered with the names of men from the Seminole Creek Nation from Seminole, Oklahoma, who served in World War I and World War II. The inscriptions record the wars the men served in, Gold Star soldiers of both wars, and where the soldiers from World War II were assigned at the time the quilt was made.

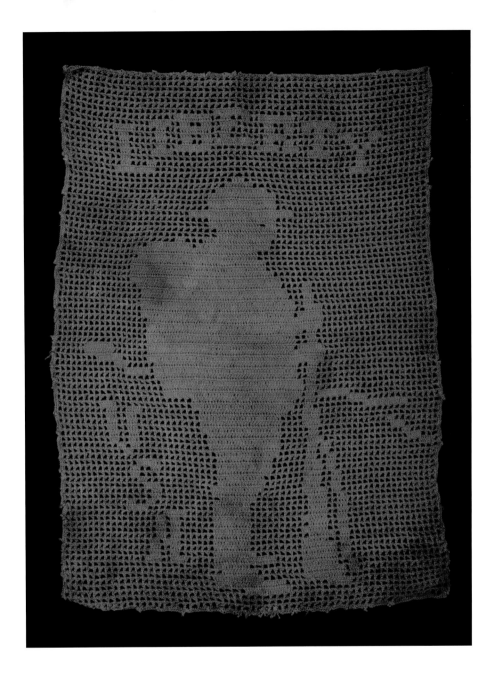

Like most of my previous books, this book combines two collections: quilts from World War I and the 1910s, and contemporaneous newspaper articles about quiltmaking. These articles historically anchor the quilts and provide sound knowledge and insight into quiltmakers of the time and the conditions affecting their lives.

I would like to thank Barbara Garrett for her assistance in photography, and Schiffer Publishing, Ltd., for their support and encouragement in the preparation of this book. Unless otherwise indicated, the quilts are included in my collection.

Lastly, I would like to share a letter published in the "What Is My Duty" September 1917 issue of *Today's Housewife*. It is a timeless, sincere, and accurate representation of the heart and soul of the mothers of the men and women who serve our country in the United States military.

Mrs. Mary Roberts Rinehart

Quoted from "The Altar of Freedom," Mrs. Rinehart's great expression of her war experiences.

Men fight wars, but it is the mothers of a nation who raise the army. They are the silent patriots. Given her will, every mother in this great land would go to war, if by doing so she could keep her sons in safety. It is easier to go than to send a boy.

Yet war is not necessarily death. I try to comfort myself with this. Perhaps it will help other mothers. It is a hazard, but it is a thing of vast rewards and much cheerfulness, of democracy, of big moments and little feasts, of smiles and grumbling, of labor and rest, and of that joy in his own kind that only the boy knows. And underneath it all, buried deep and never articulated, is that feeling of doing his bit for his country which is the foundation of which a nation rests secure.

I wish I could always remember these things. I have panicky times when the sun dies for me, and the world goes black. But I am like the other mothers. I shall go through with it, and I would not have things otherwise. He is still in his 'teens, but he is a man, and this is his country. I have not raised him to be a shirker.

1. QUILTING THROUGH THE 1910S

C. Cole Philips, Fadeaway Girl, 1912. C. Cole Philips was a popular illustrator for American magazines from 1907 to his premature death in 1927. His artistic renderings were noted for his use of "negative space," in which his beautiful women are featured dressed in clothing that either matched or disappeared into the background of the work. Here, the neat clean Basket Quilt featured on the four poster bed reflects the changing styles of the bedroom in the 1910s.

Postcard c. 1915 Fireman with Tobacco Flannel Quilt. Tobacco Flannel quilts were very popular in the first and second decades of the twentieth century.

Quiltmaking in the 1910s can be best described as the convergence of the quiltmaking styles of the late nineteenth century with the new, innovative styles of the early twentieth century. Redwork, Crazy quilts, and Multitudinous-pieced quilts, the most popular designs of the nineteenth century, were still in high favor. Cigar silk and Tobacco flannel quilts were all the rage, with appeal to the men who purchased the inhalants and to their wives who acquired the flannels which were actually marketing textiles for quilts. Two-color quilts, introduced around the turn of the twentieth century, became the more popular and fashionable choice of bed covering styles. Satin and polished cotton, wholecloth quilts offered high-end choices for the boudoir. Church and civic groups gathered to embroider Fund Raising quilts with thousands of signatures in a multitude of designs to provide

13

Postcard featuring the ideal bedroom of the time, dated March, 1912.

Postcard dated September 12, 1918. Inscribed on the back "Dear Mother, We have been moved out of here got our first shots today. I have a might sore arm already will write more as soon as my arm gets a little better. I'm feeling fine. Frank; 23rd Co. 164 D.B. Funston."

Fort Wayne News and Sentinel, Fort Wayne, Indiana, October 11, 1918, page 20.

a major source of revenue. A phenomenon new to the twentieth century was the emergence of major entrepreneurial quilt designers. The Wilkinson Sisters, Ruby Short McKim, Marie Webster, and Rosie O'Neill's Kewpies made their quiltmaking debuts with overwhelming appeal to the quilters of all ages.

Handkerchief from World War I.

The 1910s was a dynamic decade in quiltmaking featuring holdovers of the previous century and the fresh, crisp, clean bed coverings of the new century. Two catastrophic events toward the end of the decade interrupted the emergence of the newer trends in quiltmaking. World War I, also referred to as the "Great War," and the 1918 pandemic flu, also referred to as "The Spanish Flu," brought hardship and death to America, and the entire world. Much of the quiltmaking from April 1917 to March 1919 was focused on providing for our soldiers and the Red Cross. The pandemic flu also took a tremendous toll on quiltmaking and textiles in other ways. Due to the lack of knowledge about germs and disease transmission, the quilts of many sickbeds were destroyed by fire to halt the advance of a killing illness. The exact numbers of cotton quilts lost because of the sanitizing efforts from "The Spanish Flu" can never be quantified.

During the 1910s an abundance of fabrics was still evident in quiltmaking. American

The American Printing Company, where cotton fabric is dyed and printed. The Fall River Iron Works Company, "where cotton fabric is woven," as featured in the company's trade catalog, c. 1910.

Indigo Blue and White, 24 inches wide. "Our Indigo and White is the best 64x64 print cloth, warranted dyed with pure Indigo, and absolutely fast color. After being dyed, attractive patterns in White are produced upon it by printing an oxidizing agent, which when passed through a chemical bath, cuts or removes the Indigo wherever it has been printed, leaving the pure White of the fabric to form the pattern in White on the Indigo." American Printing Company catalog, c. 1910.

"Calcutta Light Blue and White, 24 inches wide. "Our Calcutta Light Blue and White fabric is the best 64x64 print cloth, dyed and printed in a manner similar to our Indigo Blue and White, except that it is dyed a lighter shade of color that looks rich and attractive with the patterns in White printed upon it. The great care exercised in the dyeing makes our Plain Shade Calcutta of exceptional value. This fabric receives special attention in the finishing, on account of its delicate shade, and the finished pieces have much the effect of silk." American Printing Company catalog, c. 1910.

"Dyed Reds, 24 inches wide. Our Dyed Reds are the best 64x64 print cloth, dyed with a pure color, guaranteed to be absolutely fast. Our process of dyeing is such that a uniformity of shade is produced rarely obtainable in this class of dyeing. We are printing this fabric with patterns in White on Red, Black on red, and Black and White on Red. Our Plain Shade of Red is particularly desirable." American Printing Company catalog, c. 1910.

"Dyed Clarets, 24 inches wide. Our Dyed Clarets are the best 64x64 print cloth, dyed a rich color with pure dyes, guaranteed to be absolutely fast. This a standard shade of color, and we spare no expense in making it the best that can be produced. Patterns in White, especially adapted for this class of work, are printed upon these Clarets in an artistic manner. Our Plain Shade is unsurpassed." American Printing Company catalog, c. 1910.

Printing Company of Fall River, Massachusetts, was the largest printer of cotton in the world. At the beginning of the second decade of the twentieth century, the manufacturer employed 6,000 workers.[1] A catalog representing the printwork's products illustrates the vast array of patterns and color combinations popular for sewing and quiltmaking in the 1910s.

Although women were still hand-piecing and hand-quilting their quilts, they were also utilizing both treadle and electric sewing machines. The average examiner really cannot detect the difference in stitches produced by foot power versus electric power. Affordability and availability of electric power dictated upgrading to the newest sewing devices and, when their financial circumstances allowed, women did not hesitate to improve their situations as seamstresses and quiltmakers.

The Boye Needle Case (c. 1910) hung in dry goods stores across the United States. Needle sizes for approximately ninety-five sewing machines are featured on the face of the Boye case, verifying that women had access to a large variety of sewing machines.

"Greys, 24 inches wide. Our success with Greys has been unprecedented. They are the best 64x64 print cloth twice printed; first for the pattern in Black and White; second to produce the cover, which gives the all-over Silver Grey appearance. The Black used is Aniline Black, and the white is produced by printing a preparation that acts as a resist to the Black of the second or cover printing. The color is absolutely fast." American Printing Company catalog, c. 1910.

"Shirtings, 24 inches wide. Our Shirtings are a selected 64x64 print cloth. We have an extensive line of both strictly staple and fancy designs, in Black, Pink, Blue, and other desirable colors. The fabric after being printed is passed through steam boxes to develop and give permanency to the colors rendering them absolutely fast. It is then washed, starched and calendared." American Printing Company catalog, c. 1910.

This c. 1914 box of Cheney Silk squares was packaged and sold specifically for the making of Crazy quilts.

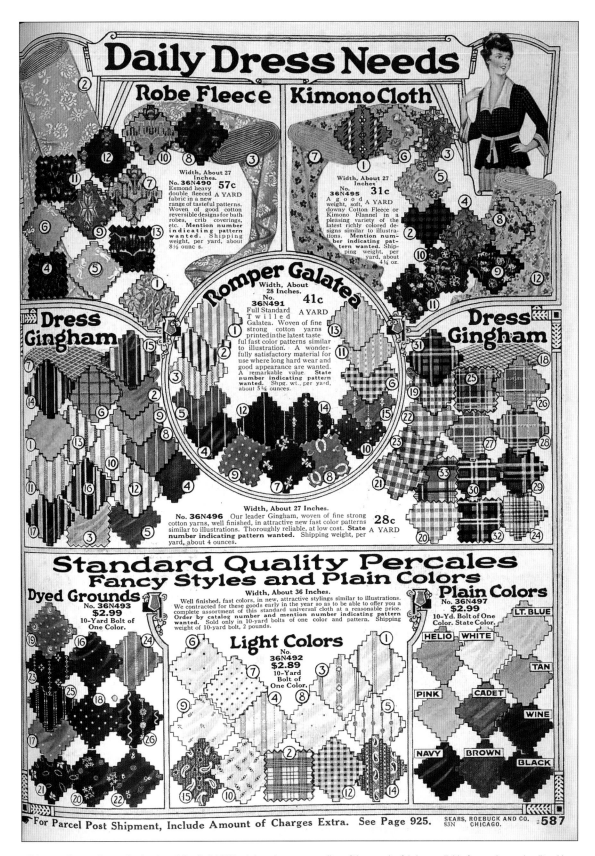

This page from a Sears, Roebuck and Co. Fall 1917 catalog shows a sampling of the popular fabrics available for sewing and quiltmaking at the beginning of U.S. involvement in World War I. HistoricCatalogsofSearsRoebuckandCo18961993_187646369, www.ancestry.com

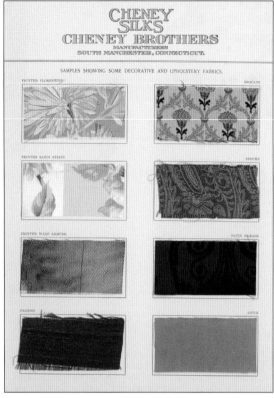

1914 Salesman's Sample, Cheney Brothers Silk, South Manchester, Connecticut.

Treadle sewing machine postcard postmarked Sept. 25, 1917.

Electric sewing machine ad, *The Saturday Evening Post*, September 7, 1918, page 81.

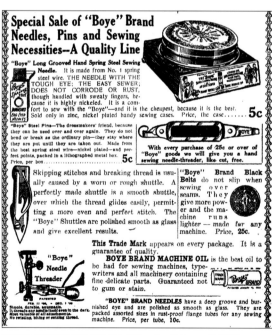

Omaha World Herald, Omaha, Nebraska, February 3, 1915, page 5.

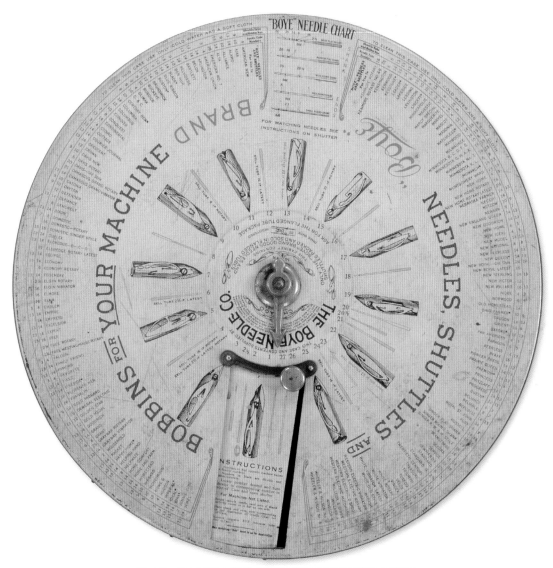

Boye Needle Holder, c. 1910, features 110 sewing machines available
in the first quarter of the twentieth century for the American housewife.

Repository
Canton, Ohio
November 6, 1910, page 36

Revival of Old-fashioned Quilting

Only a few years ago it was not un-
common sight to see a group of
women seated about a large frame,
working with all their might, tying
knots and sewing and chatting with
each other. This was the quilting party
of other days, and this sewing art is
probably the only remaining one of our
great-grandmothers. Quilting is now having a revival. Women are again taking

it up, and the patchwork quilt will soon
be as popular as it ever was. But the
quilting revival is no fad. It will last
longer than the present fad for the old-
fashioned rag carpets. Of course, quiltmaking of the twentieth century lacks
much of the old time pristine romance
because of its settings. To the gentle
woman of other days the quilting fes-
tivities were ranked among the real pleas-
ures in the restful Colonial days of hospitality.

The quilts of our great-grandmothers,
after lying for years in the cedar chests,

21

"The Quilting Party," Wallace Nutting, Colonial Revival, painted photograph, c. 1915. Wallace Nutting was a minister and artist noted for his hand-tinted photographs of staged New England interiors, homes and gardens. His works evoked the warmth and comfort of the Colonial life-style and contributed to the popularity of the Colonial revival of the early twentieth century.

Article, *Idaho Statesman*, Boise, Idaho, August 21, 1910, page 11.

have been taken out and now rank with the other treasures of the household. In the days when these quilts were made Milady, whether a noble woman or of lowly degree, was skilled in the art of using the needle. The bed coverings, made as they were from patches of all sorts and designs, were indeed works of art, each stitch a masterpiece in itself. In many of the old time quilts no two stitches were alike in form or color, and they might well be termed "crazy quilts."

For some reason the women of now have paused in the rush to take up the

bygone art of yesterday, and feminine fingers are again growing nimble at knotting, sewing and threading needles about the quilting frame. Scraps and patches are again being arranged into intricate patterns such as "The California Tree," "The Tulip," "The Log Cabin" and "The Sunrise." Patterns of 75 and 100 years ago are being closely followed, and the same arrangement of the vari-colored patches is being adopted.

In the olden times, months and even years were taken up in the making of a quilt, especially when such a complicated design as the "Tulip" is followed. The leisure moments, though they be many, are hardly enough to allow much work to be finished in a short time, and Milady of Today finds she has too little time to work her quilt when it is once started and the work becomes interesting. Quilting is quite as intrinsic as the making of blocks or squares. There are few women of today who understand

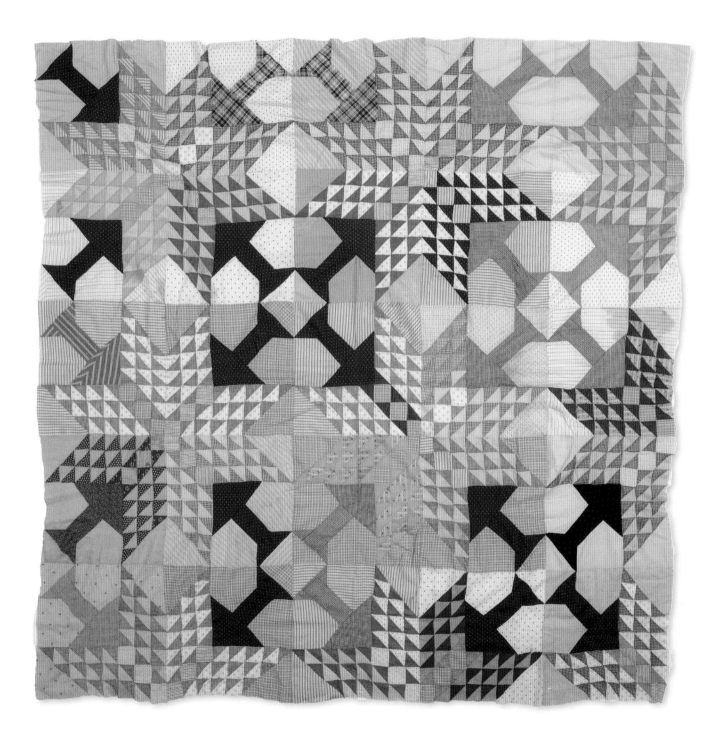

Tree of Paradise Quilt Top, c. 1910, 82 inches x 82 inches, hand pieced, cotton. This scrappy, pieced quilt is a great example of the fabrics and pattern preference of the second decade of the twentieth century.

the method of quilting and the elaborate stitches used in the old days, unless she has inherited a liking for the work and has learned it from mother or grand-mother. But, on the other hand, if one is energetic and searches hard and long she may find some quaint old colors or patterns.

Probably the most popular design of quilt is the "Log Cabin." This pattern is quite simple, but not altogether easy-to make. The patches are arranged in blocks, the similar ones at the top, gradually dropping to the longer and larger ones at the bottom. Many of these sets of blocks are found in a sin-gle quilt. The origin of the "Log Cabin" quilt is a mystery, swallowed up in the past, but it has shown that patterns of this variety came over in the Mayflower.

"The Tree of Paradise" is another favorite pattern, outside of the appliqué class. It is made of triangle-shaped pieces of green chambray gingham alter-nating with white, cut uniformly with the green. Next comes the "Sunrise" pattern of yellow-oil calico, combined with white. "The Tulip" pattern is such a complicated one that a beginner in the work will hardly undertake it.

Debutantes, as well as the girls in the colleges, have taken up the fad of quilt-ing, "Fudge parties" have given way to "quilting bees," as they are some-times called. The girl who has had sev-eral seasons in society has found time to copy one or more of these old quilts to add to the linen and lace lingerie in her "treasure chest." But probably the most amazing thing about the quilts is that they are used on the outside of the bed, and they have quite superseded the cover of ruffled Swiss or the counter-pane. Where they harmonize with the decorations nothing could be prettier in the home. The snowy pillowcases, not shams, trimmed with heavy crocheted linen lace and showing a tiny raised letter or monogram are indeed a fitting accomplishment to the quilts of our great-grandmothers.

Fancy stitches tend a great deal to-ward making the old-time quilt attract-tive. These stitches are in such num-bers that there is no need for the quilter to originate her own. Then, with the different colors of embroidery cotton, the effect of the blocks and their bor-ders is unique. Many women prefer to use a different stitch around each block of the quilt. This, of course, makes a great deal of extra work, but the re-sult pays for the time taken up. All sorts of zig-zag lines, curves, blocks, triangles, flowers and odd designs form stitches, and the sewing on of these is a feature in itself. Often, a stitch is made in two colors, one half in one and the remainder in another color. Then the thread can be blended with the other material.

Ad, *Seattle Daily Times*, Seattle, Washington, October 9, 1910, page 16.

THE FIRST NATIONWIDE QUILT COMPETITION

In the fall of 1910, the first organized, nationwide quilt contest was held in the United States. Goodin Reid & Company, a quilt batting company from Cincinnati, Ohio, sponsored "The Reddisode Revolutionary Quilt Contest." Entrance rules required the quiltmaker be a descendent of the "Sons of Battle" in the American Revolution. Newspapers across the nations published notices such as the one appearing in the *Charleroi Mail*, Charleroi, Pennsylvania, on October 1, 1910: "Not necessarily the best from an intrinsic standpoint, but best in design—best in construction—perhaps the oldest—the quilt with the most interesting historical association. YOU MAY ENTER THEM FREE and if you will phone us, we will gladly have our wagon call for any entries you desire to make."[2] A later article in the *Charleroi Mail* reported 29 quilts made by "grandmothers of years ago" were entered and exhibited at J. W. Berryman & Sons, a local department and dry goods store.

The Wolf & Dessaur Department Store in Fort Wayne, Indiana, ran an ad in the *Fort Wayne Sentinel* on Wednesday, November 2, 1910. Quilt contest specifications were incorporated directly in the ad indicating the wide-ranging scope of the competition. The notice stated, "We want some woman in Fort Wayne to win the first prize, which is now being contested for by women all over the country." The elimination process can best be described by the following article that appeared in the *Elkhart Daily Review*, Elkhart, Indiana, on September 29, 1910:

Quilt Judges Have Trouble
Find That Big Array Presents Perplexing Problem to make Decisions—Four Are Named.

Mrs. Norman Sage, Mrs. A.J. Moody and Mrs. O.C. Hill, who acted as judges in the quilt contest conducted by the Warren Hill Co., spent all of Wednesday afternoon examining the quilts and agreed that the task was much more difficult than they expected, because of the rare beauty and excellent workmanship of all the quilts.

The final decision was in favor of Mrs. C.S. Sanders of No. 122 Howland avenue, her quilt being judged the most elaborate in workmanship, while its historic value lies in the fact that it was owned by Mrs. Sanders' great-great-grandmother.

A quilt belonging to Mrs. Elmer Bowers of Osceola was chosen for fine work, while for age a quilt owned by Mrs. Klinefellter was designated. Photographs of these four quilts will be sent to Cincinnati, where they will be entered in the national quilt contest for the $500 in prizes offered by the manufacturers of the Reddisode cotton batt.

In Connecticut, the Howland Dry Goods Company of Bridgeport hosted the Reddisode competition. The three top choices from Connecticut went on to Cincinnati to be further judged. First place in Connecticut went to Mrs. C. P. Dimick of Bridgeport for a quilt design called "Washington Army." "It has all the requirements of: First, historical interest; second, age, and third, artistic beauty." Second place was conferred upon Mrs. W. F. Platt of Milford for an appliqué quilt with a "pattern so padded with cotton that the flowers and leaves are raised." Third place went to the Mariner's Compass quilt. Other Connecticut contenders were recorded as Washington's Plume, Rising Sun, Old Maid's Patience, and Bow-Knot. It was the Mariner's Compass quilt owned by Mrs. Otis B. Curtis (Harriet) of Stratford, Connecticut, that won first place in a nationwide quilt competition called "The Reddisode Revolutionary Quilt Contest."[3]

The winning Mariner's Compass quilt was originally made by Mary A. Beers of Stratford, Connecticut. Mary's grandfather, Silas, served in the Revolutionary War as a drummer in the Fifth Connecticut Regiment, sounding the march

at the Battle of Fort Ticonderoga. Her father, Silas (also recorded as Cyrus) Beers, was born in Stratford in 1792. The quilt was passed down in the family to Harriet Curtis. It was Harriet who presented the quilt for the 1910 nationwide contest.

The following congratulatory letter and a listing of the thirty winners nationwide were printed in the *Bridgeport Post*, acknowledging the quilt owned by Mrs. Otis B. Curtis of Stratford, Connecticut as the national first-place winner.

> The store and old Stratford win Reddisode quilt contest. This is an unusually merry Christmas for Mrs. Otis B. Curtis of Stratford. Yesterday, we had the pleasure of handing her a check for $100, the amount of the first prize in the Reddisode Revolutionary quilt contest conducted by Goodin Reid & Co. of Cincinnati. A quilt owned by Mrs. Curtis, exhibited at the Howland store, and selected as one of three from this city for entry in the national competition, was adjudged best of all in the country by the judges of that national competition.
>
> Over all the country from Oklahoma to Pennsylvania and from Georgia to the state of Washington, Bridgeport and Stratford hold the lead. Mrs. Curtis's handsome entry was placed at the head of the list. She was given the first prize. Seattle was second, Decatur, Ill., was third—but Mrs. Curtis was first. Not another New England contestant received a prize. Bridgeport was the only place east of New York to be among the winners. This time, we lead not alone Connecticut but all New England.

Also of interest is the Reddisode batting manufactured by Goodin Reid. A descriptive in the *Fort Wayne Sentinel* ad provides a very recognizable image of this product. "Because as the name denotes, the cotton is stitched all in one big piece—the full size of the comfort (72 x 84) and is stitched in parallel lines, three inches apart, so that when you put on the covering you will not be bothered with PUCKERINGS OR THIN PLACES and you can make your bed coverings without the cumbersome old quilting frame."

Mariners Compass Quilt, c. 1850. Made by Mary A. Beers, Bridgeport, Connecticut, 92.5 inches x 95.5 inches, cotton. This quilt won first place in what was probably the first organized, national quilt competition, the Reddisode Revolutionary Quilt Contest, sponsored by the Goodwin, Reid & Co. Batting company form Cincinnati, Ohio, in 1910.

Prize Winners Revolutionary Quilt Contest Conducted by Goodin Reid & Co., Cincinnati, Ohio
1 thru 30 below.

1. Mrs. Otis B. Curtis, $100.00 Stratford, Conn.
2. Mrs. Morgart $75.00 2121 23d Ave. So. Seattle, Wash.
3. Mrs. Alex McIntosh $50.00 1059 W. Macon St. Decatur, Ill.
4. Mrs. G.D. Craig $25.00 48 Jackson St., Grand Rapids, Mich.
5. Mrs. L.B.C. Brundage $25.00 715 W. 47th St. Los Angeles, Cal.
6. Mrs. Elenor Sage $15.00 Arcata, Cal.
7. Miss E. Robinson $15.00 Lancaster, Pa.
8. Miss E.I. Chamberlain $15.00 Amos, Iowa
9. Mrs. U.S. Shoaff $15.00 953 Columbia Ave., Ft. Wayne, Ind.
10. Mrs. C.E. Corwin $15.00 Chehalis, Wash.
11. Mrs. C.E. Douglass $10.00 Quincy, Mich.
12. Mrs. Janice Hood $10.00 Marionville, Mo.
13. Miss Gertrude Sprout $10.00 Enid, Okla.
14. Mrs. Tuttle $10.00 Zion City, Ill.
15. Mrs. F.C. Smith $10.00 Butler, Mo.
16. Mrs. Lucinda Wimer $10.00 Damont, In.
17. Samuel Hollenheck $10.00 Homey, Mich.
18. Mrs. Ida Poynter $10.00 Namps, Idaho
19. Mrs. Day $10.00 Bellaire, O.
20. Mrs. L.N. Foster $10.00 Richmond, Va.
21. Mrs. M. Downey $5.00 Yuma, Ariz.
22. Mrs. S.H. Cook $5.00 McDonald, Pa.
23. Miss Martha Morledge $5.00 Minerva, Ohio
24. Mrs. Ida McLaughlin $5.00 Sheriden, Mo.
25. Mrs. W.R. Houston $5.00 West Point, Ga.
26. Mrs. Nannie Lee $5.00 Troy, Idaho
27. Mrs. A.W. Cone $5.00 Roy, Wash.
28. Mary E. Whigin $5.00 Walton, N.Y.
29. Mrs. Frank Fisk $5.00 Union City, Mich.
30. Mrs. W.D. Grove $5.00 Marysville, Cal.[4]

The October 1911 *Pictorial Review* featured this two-page spread about a quilt exhibit sponsored by The Comfort Club. New and old quilts from around the country were shown with recognition ribbons awarded to the favorites.

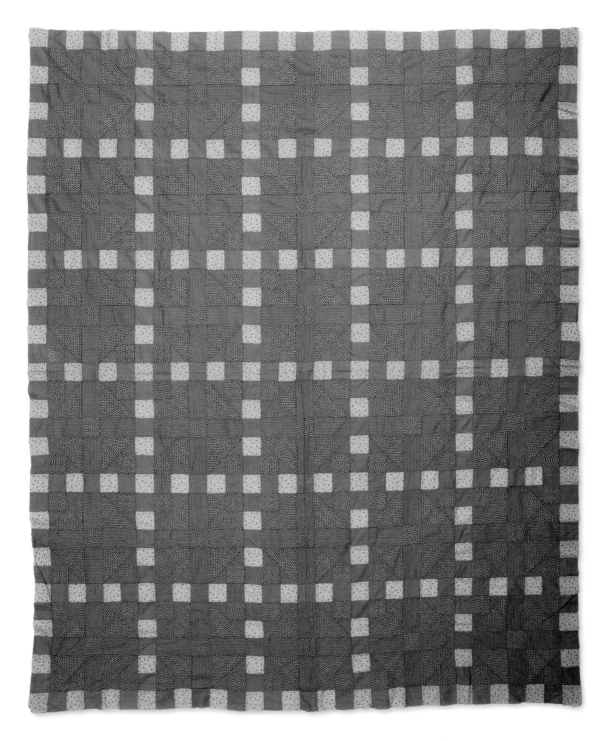

Ducks Foot Quilt Top, a Hearth and Home pattern, c. 1910, 72 inches x 78 inches, cotton.
This quilt features the bright colors of the 1910s.

Cleveland Gazette
Cleveland, Ohio
September 3, 1910, page 1
Using Up Old Ribbons.

Have you a lot of bows, sashes, and hat trimmings that are too faded and shabby for further use? Rip out all the stitches, clean off all spots, press all wrinkles and then put them into a dye pot with silk dye.

If you select ribbon of nearly the same color and same quality to go in the pot at one time you should have enough good looking ribbon to make nice plaited frills for the winter petticoat.

These dyed ribbons can also be utilized as color linings, facings or in making a patchwork quilt. For such permanent work, however, it is better not to dye as it sometimes rots silk. Wash ribbon carefully and use the best bits.

Times-Picayune
New Orleans, Louisiana
January 8, 1911, page 43
An Easy Bedquilt

Cold weather is here with a vengeance and some of us are wishing we had one of the heavy quilts grandmother handed down to us and we handed down—to the church fair. Well, here is the way to make one quickly and easily.

Get two pieces of sateen or of mercerized printed goods in contrasting yet harmonious colors, and of the proper size to fit your bed. Put the right sides together and machine stitch up two of the sides. Then turn the goods inside out and run it up in stripes six inches apart.

Next get a soft calico, which tear up into strips each six inches wide. Machine stitch these up the sides and fill them with cotton batting.

Trade Card for Singer Sewing Machine No. 15-30.

The Suffragette postcard series was published from about 1909 through the 1910s. In a humorous way, they reflected upon the women's suffrage movement which began in Britain. Women of both countries were influenced by society's quest for equality for women. During World War I, women primarily focused their attention in raising funds to support American and British troops. Their strength and participation on the homefront helped to turn the tide of public opinion in their favor and furthered their quest for equality after the war.

Draw the cotton-filled calico into the strips of your quilt, being sure to fit them evenly and neatly, and sew up the ends. Finish with a ribbon quilt or edging and your quilt is done.

Coshocton Daily Age
Coshocton, Ohio
July 15, 1911, page 5
Mrs. Gamble Hostess of Missionary Society

The July meeting of the Warsaw Presbyterian Missionary Society was held at the home of Mrs. Gamble Thursday afternoon. The ladies brought their thimbles and pieced quilt blocks for the missionary barrel to be sent this fall. A short program was given following which a bounteous picnic supper was served on the lawn. There were over forty members in attendance.

Cleburne Morning Review
Cleburne, Texas
January 28, 1912, page 4
A Grand Success.

The Senior League of Brazos Avenue Methodist church gave a measuring party at the home of Mrs. Lona Allen No. 906 E. Henderson street, on Thursday night, which was largely attended by folks from one year to fifty years old, and at which everyone had the "time of their lives."

The purpose of this social was to auction off a quilt which they had made to raise money to pay on the church debt. The quilt was of an odd design, having nine wheels pieced in the colors, red, white and blue, with twenty nine names on each square, for which they realized $40. 05. From the measuring they received $15. 10, and the quilt was sold for $7.15. The grand total raised by the league was the handsome sum of $62.30. This shows that energies turned in the right channels will produce the harvest. Many thanks to all contributors.

Emporia Gazette
Emporia, Kansas
August 5, 1912, page 1
State Suffrage Work

Bazaars are no new feature in feminine annals. Mrs. Grinstead held one recently at

31

Flying Geese Quilt top, c. 1910, 71 inches x 80 inches, cotton.
The indigo blues and shirting prints in this quilt reflect the popular fabric choices of the time.

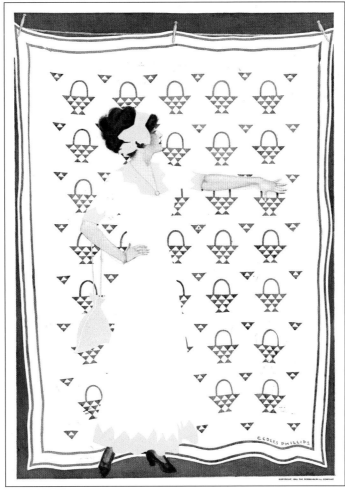

C. Cole Philips, Fadeaway Girl, 1912. Baskets were a favored pattern for early twentieth century quilts. Typical of the trademark style of C. Cole Philips, the image of the early-twentieth-century lady fades into the background quilt.

Liberal for campaign expenses. She cleared $10. One object of especial interest was a quilt pieced for the suffrage cause by Grandmother Patrick, who is nearly 92 years old.

National Labor Tribune
Pittsburgh, Pennsylvania
August 15, 1912, page 6
An Asbestos Pad.
An asbestos pad for the table may be made in this way: Get enough asbestos paper to cover the table with double thickness. From a couple of old sheets cut two pieces the size of the table. Baste the asbestos paper between them and quilt it in the sewing machine, using a long stitch. This is necessary, as the paper tears and pulls apart easily. Put this pad on the table under your silence cloth, and there will be no marks made on the polished surface by hot dishes.

Plaindealer
Topeka, Kansas
August 16, 1912, page 2
Newton, Kansas
The C.M.E. ladies of the sewing circle pieced a quilt and sent it to Wichita to a gentleman, who has a quilting machine, who did the quilting free. The quilt was beautiful

and to dispose of it the circle selected the following ladies to enter a contest to see who could raise the largest amount to receive the quilt: Mrs. G. C. Granbury 0; Mrs. C. Riley 15c; Mrs. A.J. Tandy 85c; Mrs. Wm. Slaughter $1.40; Mrs. U.S. Rickman $5.70; Mrs. A.L. Turner $10.19; Mrs. J.M. Gross $16.20; total $34.49: Mrs. Gross having raised the largest amount was awarded the quilt.

Patriot
Harrisburg, Pennsylvania
October 2, 1912, page 2

This Quilt Has
16,000 Patches

Policeman Carson's Grand-
mother Made It Many
Years Ago

Each A Half Inch Long

Policeman Oscar Carson yesterday issued a challenge to any person who can present a quilt containing more patches than the one which he now possesses. This quilt, the officer said, contains more than 16,000 patches. Several weeks ago a story appeared in a local newspaper of a man who claimed that he was possessor of a prize quilt and issued a challenge to any person who could present one containing more patches. That quilt, according to the story, was made of 10,000 patches.

The quilt, which Policeman Carson owns, was made by his grandmother, Mrs. Rachel Carson, a number of patches in triangular shape and about a half an inch in length. After her death, the quilt which is about five feet square, was presented to the officer. Carson never paid any particular attention to the number of patches in his quilt, or even thought that it was a prize winner, until the article appeared in the newspaper.

Portsmouth Daily Times
Portsmouth, Ohio
February 4, 1913, page 1

AGED WOMAN GIVES
PRES. TAFT A QUILT.

(By Associated Press.)

Washington, D.C., Feb. 4.—President Taft's collection of gifts was increased today when he received a red, white, and blue quilt from Mrs. H.C. Reed, Merna Neb., 82 years old, who wrote the quilt had been made entirely by hand and contained 5,082 separate stitches.

Richmond Times Dispatch
Richmond, Virginia
March 1, 1913, page 10

1,600 PIECES OF SILK IN QUILT.

Will be presented to President-Elect and
Mrs. Wilson.

Fredericksburg, Va., February 28.—A quilt, the work of Charles Miller, of Philadelphia, a native of Germany, but for over half a century a citizen of this country, and family of this city, has been completed. It is intended as a gift from Mr. Miller to President-elect and Mrs. Wilson. It contains 1,600 patches of silk, some in the colors of Old Glory, others in the Princeton orange and black, a few in dark red and navy, the colors of Germany. Typical of the White House, is an attractive counter-design in white.

Mr. Miller is eighty-two years of age and has made the quilt entirely by hand since Christmas. Mr. Miller resided in Fredericksburg years ago, and is well known to many citizens. He visits here nearly every summer. Mr. Miller exhibited a remarkable quilt at the last Fredericksburg Fair, which attracted much attention. It was of many pieces and made entirely by hand by Mr. Miller himself.

Eight Point Star, c. 1915, 68 inches x 76 inches, cotton. These patriotic red, white and blue fabrics are the colors of the World War I era.

Fan Quilt, c. 1910, 81 inches x 90 inches, cotton. Hundreds of fabrics from the late nineteenth and early twentieth centuries were pieced into this fan quilt. Fans were another very popular design chosen by women of the early twentieth century for quilts.

Richmond Times Dispatch
Richmond, Virginia
March 9, 1913, page 45

PATCHWORK REVIVAL

Many who love tradition and the arts followed by gentlewoman of yore will be happy to learn that the old-fashioned patchwork has been revived. The "quilting bee" will again be numbered among the fashionable entertainments. So search the attic for the quilting frames, which have become dusty poked away in a corner since grandmother's day. Haul out your patch bags and find the scraps of material left from Nelly's or Sue's frocks and start to patch Peggy a quilt for her dower chest.

When you have pieced the required number of blocks then invite your friends to the "quilting bee," which is always followed by an elaborate supper and party.

<text>When deciding to piece your quilt, select material of the same variety and quality, like gingham, chambray, percale or linen. Choose your design, and from oddly-shaped scraps cut a large number of small patches using a pattern to secure uniformity in shape.

From unbleached muslin cut squares to be used for a foundation on which to build the design. For instance, if you choose to piece a fan quilt, cut a piece of material of a plain color in the shape of a quarter circle and stitch it across one corner of the square. four patched radiate from this to form a half fan, which, when joined to a similar block, completes the semicircle and the fan.

When the required number of blocks are finished, join them together, forming the large top of the quilt, and line with a layer of cotton. Over this stitch the lining, and the quilt is ready for quilting.

The proper lines for quilting the fan design run from its centre through the sections of the fan. Attach the quilt to a frame and sew with a running stitch, using white thread and a long needle. The thread should be rather coarse to insure strength.

Patch work offers great possibilities for color schemes and original designing. Some of the designs on our heirloom quilts are extremely intricate, namely, the star of Bethlehem, apple tree, log cabin, basket of flowers, and the butterfly.

Patriot
Harrisburg, Pennsylvania
June 20, 1913, page 4

Nursery Quilts

Distinctive quilts for the little tots' room are a joy to the children and a delightful task for mothers. They are very expensive if bought and less individual of course. Here are a few ideas for home-made designs that will make nursery quilt things to be remembered in after years, besides being present joys.

The flower quilt always holds great attraction for youngsters. If the nur-

The Modern Priscilla Magazine, May 1917

37

sery be prepared in daisy paper, the carrying out of this idea is one of the easiest things imaginable. On a foundation of silk, poplin or best of all, unbleached muslin, arrange the daisies in a straight border, the stems growing from a plain band on the edge of the quilt, continuing around the four sides.

To make the daisies, cut an oval four inches long and one inch at its greatest width. Make a pattern of a petal three inches by about three-quarters of an inch. Cut out sixteen of these from white muslin if your background is a color. Make the center yellow in this case. If you are going to have yellow petals, the center should be a golden brown.

Stems in this quilt should be straight, with here and there a leaf.

Arrange the petals around the center—under it—and place the stem under one edge. Sew around the edges, without turning in, using the sewing machine or quick running stitches by hand.

This is a very attractive design, the idea being capable of many different treatments in the field of flowers. Poppies, tulips, roses, daffodils, clematis, may be used; and one flower quilt has a huge basket, upset, from which are tumbling in confusion dear to the child's heart all kinds of blossoms, that spread out to the corners of the quilt. In this pattern all colors of material are used. The variegated effect is of continuous interest to the little owner.

Boston Journal
Boston, Massachusetts
November 14, 1913, page 3
She Will Sleep
Under Cover Of
Famous Names
Mrs. Agnew's Quilt Is Most
Unique In Its Rarity.

How do you think you'd feel if you tried to sleep under the real autographs of some 300 of the most famous persons of our day? Would it keep you awake, for instance, to know that around your neck was tucked a patch bearing the real John Hancock of a famous general, and over your tootsies lay the self-penned names of half a dozen famous actresses? Would it make you cheerful mornings to wake up and meet the signature of the funniest comedian on earth with the first glance from your sleepy eyes? At any rate, it would be an experience worth recording.

This is just what will happen to Mrs. C. Rutledge Agnew of New York is doing with the unique birthday gift presented to her by Mrs. H.F. Butler. Mrs. Agnew, who is the wife of an artist with a studio at 4 West Twenty-ninth street, reached the age of 21 today. Mrs. Butler is Mrs. Agnew's grandmother, and her present was the famous patchwork quilt containing the wonderful array of autographs.

The quilt was completed by Mrs. Butler in 1906, after four years' work. It is made of ribbons, each ribbon containing a signature. The ribbons were signed in a score of countries, and each has its own story. Some were easy to get, others were obtained only after a deal of persuasion and letter writing.

Mrs. Butler made the quilt for her daughter. Because of her death it passed to Mrs. Agnew, who before her marriage was Miss Violet Gunther. The coverlet is two yards square and its entire surface is covered with autographs.

Conspicuous among the names is that of Theodore Roosevelt, which appears on a light gray ribbon fifteen inches long above the date 1902. Beneath the name of Abram S. Hewitt is the date May 27, 1902. Bishop Henry C. Potter blotted his first attempt, so that his name appears twice on the same ribbon.

Others prominent are Viola Allen, Maude Adams, Margaret Anglin, Kyrie Bellew, Amelia Bingham, Cornelius N. Bliss, Nelson Butler, Jennie Busley, Henry Miller, Edward Morgan, Julia

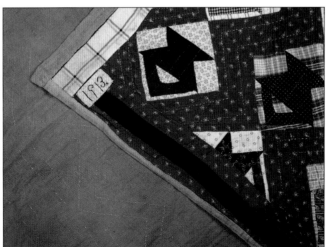

Basket Quilt, dated 1913, 84 inches x 96 inches, cotton. Made with a deep scrap bag, this quilt contains a wealth of fabric from the early twentieth century.

Marlowe, Helena Modjeska, Mary Man-
nering, Marion Manola, Louis Mann,
Burr McIntosh, Christie McDonald, Mel-
bourne McDowell, Mabel McKinley, Ben-
jamin B. Odell, Annie Oakley, Elita
Proctor Otis, Tony Pastor, Eleanor Rob-
son, Annie Russell, Stuart Robson,
Rear Admiral Schley, John P. Sousa,
Stoddart, Jennie Satterlee, Citizen
George Francis Train, Mark Twain,
Denman Thompson, John Wanamaker
and Annie Yeamans.

Only three of those whose autographs
were solicited refused. Helen Gould
declared that she was opposed to the
custom. William Gillette returned the
ribbon unsigned, and Henrietta Cros-
man offered her autograph in exchange
for $3 toward a charity in which she
was interested. The offer was accepted
by Mrs. Butler. Julia Marlowe also de-
manded a contribution for charity, Mrs.
Butler's expenses included $12 for
stamps and the cost of ribbons.

Plain Dealer
Cleveland, Ohio
November 15, 1913, page 11
Woman Conducting Quilt
Display And One Exhibit
A wonderful blue-green and yellow
peacock rests on a bough inside of
a wreath of green leaves and scarlet
blossoms. Outside are four vases of
bright hued flowers, several small pea-
cocks, some fruit and a border of
running vines and blossoms. The
whole wonderful pattern, cut out of
bright hued calicoes and sewed on
with microscopic stitches, decorates
the coverlid in which the promoters
of today's quilt show stand most in
awe.

"Some woman sewed her artistic
longings into that quilt," said Mrs.
Homer H. Johnson, one of the prime
movers in the display, which is open
from 10 a.m. to 10 p.m. today at
the College club, for the benefit of
the Wellesley endowment fund.

One hundred quilts are on view,
several of them a century or more

old, others modern adaptations of old
designs. A French cambric appliqué
quilt has 200 tiny pieces in each
block, with clusters of shiny roses
decorating the white squares between.
An autograph quilt boasts twenty-five
blocks, each by a different hand, with
an eagle and flags commemorating a
soldier of the civil war. A huge
star in the middle of another has almost the effect of a stained glass
window design, so tastefully are the
colors blended.

One quilt boasts 200 green buds
carefully stuffed. One, a "log cabin"
from Canada, is made entirely of
white stocking tops.

From Eliza Jennings home
comes a new quilt with pink, purple
and blue morning glories appliquéd
on a white ground.

Quaint old patterns are "Tulip and
Cherry," "Robbing Peter to Pay
Paul," "Wild Goose Chase," "Pine
Tree," "Feathered Star," "Pineapple,"
"Tufted Cherry," "Prince's Feather."
"Feather" borders and block corners
are marvelously quilted.

Many of the quilts are heirlooms.
All are of great value not only for
their individual interest and worth,
but as types of a bygone phase of
woman's work.

Fort Worth Star-Telegram
Fort Worth, Texas
March 3, 1914, page 5
Sewing Made Agreeable
Present methods for teaching children to sew vary as widely from those
of a generation ago as the methods
used in teaching the A B Cs or in any
other line of education. The practical
mother of today sees the necessity of
teaching her little daughter to sew just
as much as did the one of twenty-five
or fifty years ago, but today she real-
izes that there are "royal roads to
learning" this useful art and that it
may be made to appear to the little
seamstress more in the light of play
than work.

"Anna Belle Gives a Quilting Bee." *Charleston Mail*, Charleston, West Virginia, December 4, 1915, page 14.

The old fashioned way of setting a "stint" of just so long a seam, or a half hour's work, has been passed entirely by the wise mother, and she sees to it that the little girl does not become weary of her task. Memory recalls the block of the quilt that the ambitious mother required the child to piece every day, as it was thought that this methodical way of teaching sewing would also teach her to be ambitious as well. In too many cases this method did not instill in the child a love for sewing, but rather made her feel that it was an unpleasant duty that should be gotten over a soon as possible. To have pieced a large quilt of the "flat iron" pattern, before one was 7 years old was thought to be a feat to boast of by both the mother and child, although it was many times the last one that the little girl ever wanted to make, but it several its purpose in teaching her to place the stitches correctly.

By the new methods, where work and education are made so attractive that they are looked upon as play by the little students, there usually remains a sense of childish delight in the labor which was only too often looked upon with dislike when taught by the old-fashioned methods. The wise mother of today takes an interest in teaching the little daughter how to sew, and, instead of the large quilt, the very proportions of which made the work appear a mountainous task, it is easy to help the child to desire a quilt for the latest addition to the family dolls, whether it be little "Polly Pinkey" or "Miss Penelope Linkerfelter." This new favorite must, of course, have her quilt made just as nicely and the stitches as dainty as can be done, so mother is asked to cut the little squares or "flat irons" of gingham and percale and she usually bastes them together, or at least the first ones, turns back the edges evenly and explains just how the needle should be held to sew "over and over," the stitches placed and the thread drawn closely enough to held the seam firmly but not so tight that it will draw the cloth. If there is any lagging of interest in the work, the mother will lead a helping hand so that it may not last so long as to become distasteful.

After learning to sew over and over, and the quilt is finished, for a new piece of work is never begun until another has been completed, there are little petticoats and other garments to be made for Miss Dolly on which the child may learn to run seams, back stitch, hem and shirr. Not only may the actual sewing be learned, but the use of paper patterns, for all pattern companies sell dolls' patterns, and the cutting and fitting of garments in dolly's wardrobe is intensely interesting. With the cutting of the garments is also taught the lesson of care and saving of material and how the entire dress must be planned before it is cut.

Ad, *The Washington Post,* Washington D.C., April 16, 1916, page 14. The Wilkinson sisters of Ligonier, Indiana, began their cottage boudoir quilt business as World War I was strengthening in Europe. The slogan "Made in America" was already popular. The sisters responded to the newly popular, more sophisticated, yet simpler style of coverings for the bed with these elegant quilts. See the photos on pages 43 and 44.

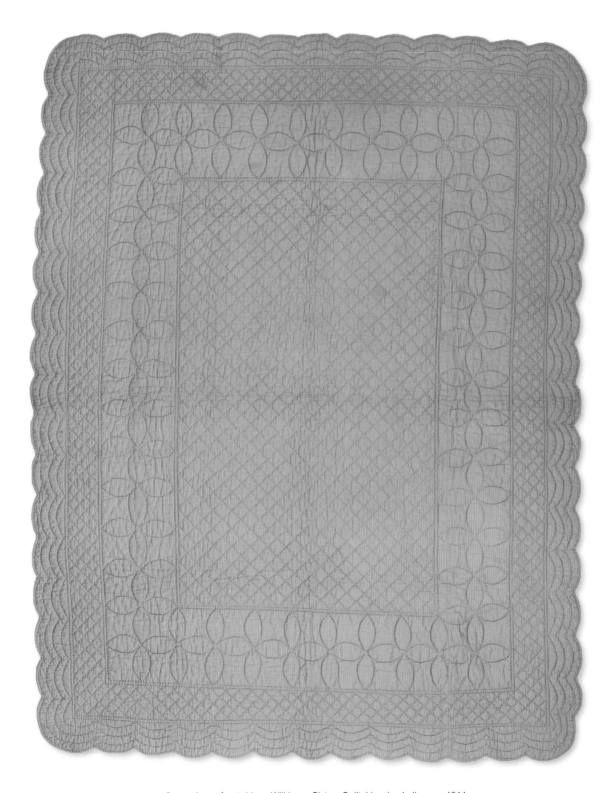

Queen Anne, front side; a Wilkinson Sisters Quilt, Ligonier, Indiana, c. 1914,
machine pieced, hand quilted, cotton. Courtesy of Marilyn Goldman.

Queen Anne, reverse side; a Wilkinson Sisters Quilt, c. 1914, machine pieced,
hand quilted, cotton. Courtesy of Marilyn Goldman.

Nashua Reporter
Nashua, Iowa
March 5, 1914, page 8
BLANKETS AND QUILTS
Best Way of caring for the
Bed Accessories.
Little Glycerin Added to the Rinse
Water is Recommended—Quilts
Liable to Fade May Be Cleaned
With Gasoline.

Quilts that are liable to fade if washed may be cleaned with gasoline. allow it to remain over night. Drain and place in a second tub of gasoline. strain the gasoline in the first tub, and use it with a fresh supply for cleaning the second piece. When washing colored quilts avoid using alkali. It will run the colors and ruin the material. If quilts are badly soiled, put kerosene in the first tub. It will cut the dirt.

Bedding washed early in the spring may be dried out of doors, but the pieces should afterward be thrown over a line hung in a room to dry thoroughly. Ticking should be soaked in water containing borax. Iron the pieces dry. If thin, coat lightly with paraffin on the wrong side. This will prevent feathers from working through.

Tampa Tribune
Tampa, Florida
April 5, 1914, page 15
Pay For Having Their
Names On A Fancy Quilt
Total Reaches $162 a Sum That Will
Be Increased When the Bed
Covering is Sold

HOYT, Kan., April 4.—The Ladies' Aid Society of the Methodist Church of this place has just completed a name quilt containing 42 blocks and 788 names of persons who contributed, the amounts ranging from ten cents to $5. Many prominent men were among the contributors among them being Arthur Capper, ex-Governor Stubbs and Bishop Quayle. The amount raised was $162.70, of

which Mrs. Amedia Dunahugh collected $40.25, and Mrs. A.C. Koser $40.

A program was given in the church, which was attended by Gov. George H. Hodges and Senator Joe Howe. Each made an address.

At the close of the program the women burned their note for $500, which they gave at the time the church was dedicated three years ago, and on which the last payment was made last week with the money received from the autograph quilt.

Bids are being received on the quilt and the ladies expect to realize quite a little sum from this source. The quilt is white each block being in the shape of a wheel and the names embroidered in red and represents a great deal of work.

Wichita Daily Times
Wichita Falls, Texas
May 31, 1914, page 4
Quilting Bee Is Held
By Just So Club Saturday

The Just So Club met at nine o'clock Saturday morning at the very pleasant home of Mrs. M. J. Gardner, for the purpose of quilting the "Philathea" quilt. Each member took a thimble and one dish for the "spread" which was enjoyed immensely at high noon. The quilt is a beauty and the club will sell it, the money to go into the Philathea treasury. It will be on display in a window down town some time in the near future. Those of the Club deserving special attention for their work are: Miss Bolton who quilted holes in her thimble; Miss Barwisse, whose left hand fitted in charmingly; Miss Downing whose strawberries fitted in charmingly also; and Mrs. Shelton, who worked hardest to earn the after dinner nap. After a delicious pineapple sherbet, the meeting adjourned with many thanks to Mrs. Gardner and family for the gracious hospitality shown. Those who attended were: Misses Edwards, Bullard, Coffield, Barwise, Bolton, Smith, Barrier, Gardner,

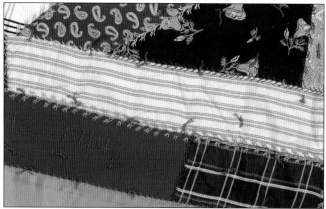

Crazy Quilt, dated 1914, 72 inches x 83 inches, hand pieced, hand embroidered, silk.
Crazy quiltmaking was still immensely popular with quiltmakers of the second decade of the twentieth century.

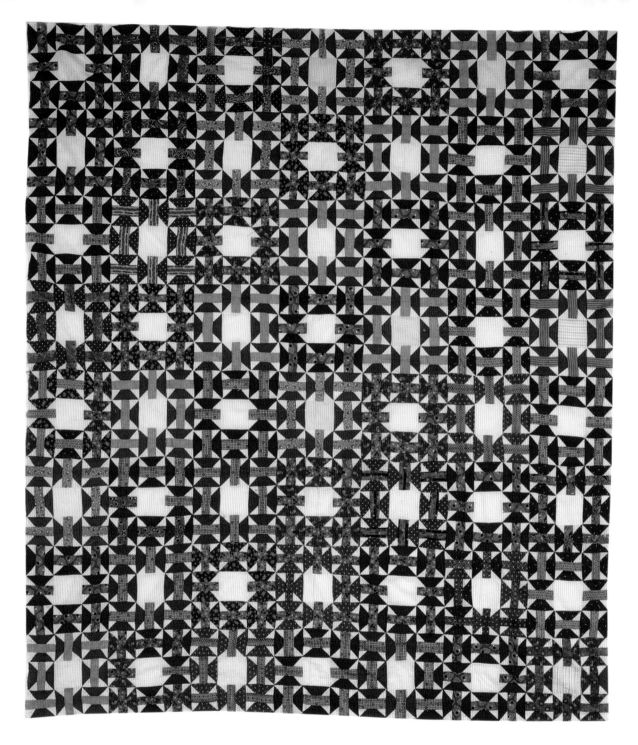

Beggar's Block or Cats and Mice Quilt top, c. 1910, 71 inches x 80 inches, cotton.
This rarely seen pattern reads as a two-color quilt featuring red and mourning prints of the era.

Wilkes, Martin, Downing, Mesdames Walker, Shelton, Bittingsley, MacDowell, Higgins, Jenne, Hartsook and Gardner.

Richmond Times Dispatch
Richmond, Virginia
September 27, 1914, page 25
Asheville Rooms

ASHEVILLE, N.C. September 26.—Capital is being added every week to the manufacturing and industrial greatness of Asheville. Now comes the announcement that the French Broad Manufacturing Company plans to install a spinning mill as an addition to its quilt mill, the latter having an annual output of 550,000 quilts. It contemplates an expenditure of about $250,000.

Galveston Daily News
Galveston, Texas
October 10, 1914, page 8

Mrs. Georgia Jackson, of Kittanning, Pa., has set a new world's record having just completed a quilt consisting of 4,540 pieces.

Oregonian
Portland, Oregon
October 17, 1914, page 8
Oregon For Quilts!

PORTLAND, Oct. 16—(To the Editor.)—In the Oregonian, October 16, is an item, "Oregon Leads on Quilts." I have a quilt with 16,339 pieces. This quilt is quilted on a sewing machine diagonally so as to form small diamonds. Stitching is five-eights inch apart. The quilt is 79 by 85 ½ inches.

Mrs. R.C. Bell, 589 Sixth Street

Galveston Daily News
Galveston, Texas
October 19, 1914, page 8
Women Can Provide
Work For Jobless
Unemployed Can Be Reinstated
In Mills if Fashionable
Buy Native Goods

There is a chance today for the women of America to display their patriotism, not as the women of Europe are focused to show theirs, by giving up homes and husbands and watching impotently the destruction of everything that has meant life and happiness to them. American women have an opportunity to conserve and foster those things which are the source of National life, the country's arts and industries and manufacturers, says the North American (Philadelphia).

They can express the highest form of patriotism, which is the promotion of public welfare.

Now as never before can the American woman show herself in her true colors. Is she a snob, an imitator, an impersonator, a picker-up of fashion's crumbs that fall from the counters of European shops? Has she lost the sturdiness and independence of her pioneer woman ancestors, who wore homespun, made on their own looms, and took pride in the industries fostered at their own firesides? Have prosperity and the slavish following of fashion deprived her of her inherited pride in America?

The European war has closed, temporarily at least, many avenues of importation. In the meantime, whether or not, the slogan, "Made in America," will take the place of the foreign trademark depends largely upon the women of the country. They are the shoppers and spenders; they create the demand which industry supplies. In the past American women have been too indifferent or too much lacking in independence to demand homemade goods and to demand that they be as well made as those coming from abroad.

The Fort Wayne Sentinel
Fort Wayne, Indiana
November 11, 1914, page 5
Outdoor Sleeping and How to Keep Warm in Winter.

On winter nights don't close your windows because you are cold but learn to keep warm with it open.

First arrange your room so that you do not sleep in a direct draught. If that is impossible the following simple method may be employed.

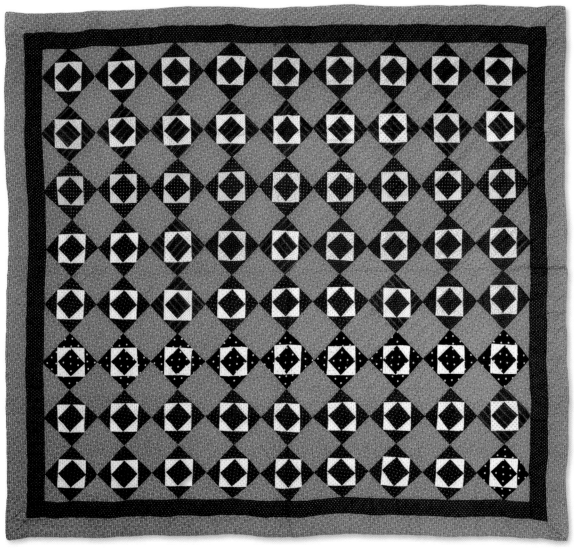

Economy Patch Quilt, c. 1915, 78 inches x 92 inches, cotton. Economy Patch was first seen
in quilts as early as the late nineteenth century. It is featured here in blue and orange, opposite colors of the color spectrum.

Cut a heavy piece of cotton six inches longer than the width of the window frame and 18 inches wide. Tack it along its lower edge to the window sill and hook the upper corners to the window frame. The windows may then be opened wide, but the current of air will be directed upwards.

Equally important is the bed. A thick mattress and pad should be sufficient under the sleeper, but if the mattress is thin, place heavy wrapping paper under it. Flannelette sheets may be used in preference to cotton. The lighter the top cover the better.

If down or lamb's wool are too expensive, a quilt made of two layers of flannelette with an interlining of newspapers will prove an excellent covering over the blankets.

For the outdoor sleeper a Klondyke bed or sleeping bag is necessary in real cold weather.

The Klondyke bed is made by tucking the blankets under the mattress-pad at feet and sides and binding the whole securely by tucking the top covering 12 inches under the mattress at foot and sides.

For stormy weather a horse blanket of quilt with a canvas covering makes an excellent protection. The bed should be heated by hot water bottles before entering it and the covering must not be so tight that the feet are uncomfortable.

Iowa City Daily Press
Iowa City, Iowa
November 23, 1914, page 5
Oldtime Needlework

Needlework is so rapidly becoming a lost art that it is in the nature of a fairy tale to explain that something like a half a century ago little girls, not especially precocious, either, learned the fundamental principles of threading a needle and pushing it through the fabric at the age of two and one-half years, and by the time they were three, pegged away at squares of patchwork, ultimately completing "quilts" for future use.

"OH! ISN'T IT NICE TO BE MARRIED?"

Postcard, postmarked 1912.

Marion Star
Marion, Ohio
March 8, 1915, page 3

When old stockings and socks are past mending, the legs are often so good and warm that it seems a pity to cast them away. Take an old sheet, cut the feet off the stockings, cut the legs open down the seam, lay them flat, and tack upon the sheet until it is all covered. Then line it with an old blanket or woolen tablecloth. The lining should if possible be woolen so as to be as warm as possible. Quilt it all together neatly, then with some bright, cheerful-looking cretonne cover the sheet, and you will have a nice warm quilt for very little cost.

Lincoln Daily News
Lincoln, Nebraska
April 9, 1915, page 16
Sateen For The New
Sunburst Quilts

We carry all shades in this sateen for making these quilts. Great care has been exercised in the selection of colors, so they will blend perfectly. If you want to start a Sunburst quilt we will be pleased to supply the necessary information and directions at the Lining Department.

Plaindealer
Topeka, Kansas
August 13, 1915, page 7
Kansas City, Kansas

The Sewing circle of the Metropolitan Baptist church held a very large meeting at the church recently and Miss Tina Calhoun sang a sweet solo; Mrs. Patterson and others discussed "Miracles" in an intelligent manner, and Miss Sherd of Oklahoma talked. The ladies are quilting a beautiful quilt, "The Texas Lily."

Repository
Canton, Ohio
August 29, 1915, page 16
Lure Of The Patchwork Quilt.

The four poster bedstead to be truly fashionable in effect now must have its old fashioned patchwork quilt. Some women are copying genuine old quilt patterns, and others are evolving patterns of their own, the colored bits of fabric being combined with plain or flowered materials in quite charming effects.

One may start a silk patchwork quilt or a cotton quilt. The former is easier to make because of the softness of the silk, but the cotton patchwork is equally smart and may be equally attractive if the pattern is well worked out. Scraps cut from old dancing frocks of pussy willow taffeta or goldenrod satin in pastel colorings make very dainty quilts for the boudoir chaise longue, the satin and taffeta fabrics in combination achieving a variety in luster, while the matching of the colors gives the color design.

Quilts of flowered and plain silk are also pleasing. One charming quilt of this kind was evolved from a castoff evening coat of pink faille classique silk in a delicate white pussy willow taffeta. The pattern was done in blocks, flowered and plain silks cut in triangles, and the blocks were joined with strips of pink satin ribbon. Such a quilt must be lined with thin cotton wadding being put between. Then, stretched over a quilting frame, the finishing touch—quilting with exquisitely fine hand stitches—is added.

Lincoln Daily News
Lincoln, Nebraska
September 3, 1915, page 12
Passion For Quilting Bee
No Home Considered Complete
Without Handsome Bit of
Ancient Work.
(By Margaret Mason.)

Good gracious, can it really be
This reason that we're going to see
The good old fashioned quilting bee
Replace the favored tango tea?
It certainly looks so to me!
NEW YORK. Sept. 3.—The newest bee in milady's bonnet is a mighty old one—the quilting bee, if you please. At least a perfect passion for this old time handwork is sweeping over the modern hearth and now no home is complete without a bit of handsome quilting. Smocking has been laid aside and patching up has become a fine art.

Several of the smart specialty shops in Fifth Avenue are showing some delightfully artistic and wondrously attractive things in the quilting line.

There are first of all the large bed quilts done on unbleached muslin with appliquéd designs of old fashioned hollyhocks in lovely rose pinks and green and the whole quilt bound in an inch wide binding of green. Then there

Sunburst Quilt Top, c. 1910, 87 inches x 87 inches, cotton. Glorious is the best descriptive for this
radiating star quilt top. Making this quilt requires special attention when cutting the diamonds in order for it to lie flat.
The photograph indicates bunching and ripples that may prevent the quilt from being successfully quilted.

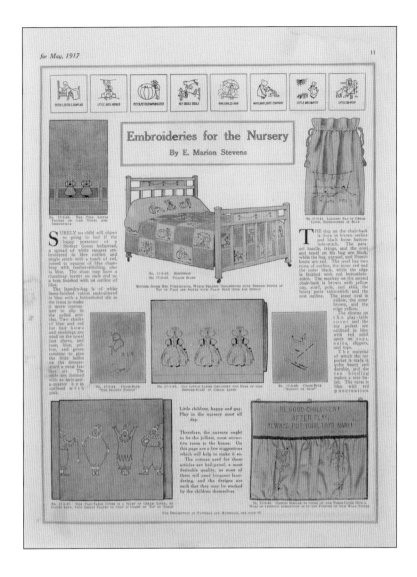

is the morning glory design in shades of blue and lavender. The hollyhock design and colors are perhaps the most effective and there are slip covers for chairs, table covers and even curtains in the same patterns the latter appliquéd on a single thickness of the muslin and quilted only in the sense of the patch work design being stitched on by hand.

Salt Lake Telegram
Salt Lake City, Utah
October 9, 1915, page 39
A Creeping Quilt
Who ever thought of it? And why did not someone think of it

sooner? What? Why, the idea of putting those linen Mother Goose books to good use. Some thinking person has conceived the idea of cutting out the Mother Goose characters from those linen books and appliquéing them on pink or blue silkaline or chambray or similar material for a baby's creeping quilt. When the youngster finds his favorite story characters under his very feet, as it were, he will not want to wander far. The idea may also be utilized for a bedquilt and will find warm welcome with the young members of the nursery.

Elkhart Daily Review
Elkhart, Indiana
December 2, 1915, page 4

Unique Quilt for Sale

The Ladies of Division No. 2 of the Ladies' League, of Church of Christ (Disciples), are offering for sale a QUILT of Oak Leaf design, and unusually attractive as well as of special value.

The design was brought from Germany by Frances Barringer 60 years ago. The pieces were all whipped on top of block in a most substantial way, notwithstanding that she is now 80 years old.

Mrs. Barringer gave the Quilt to Mrs. Denver Shreve, who, in turn gave the quilt top to this Division of which she is an active member.

The Quilt can be seen at the Division's bazaar in the Templin Music Co. window Friday and Saturday of this week.

Plain Dealer
Cleveland, Ohio
December 12, 1915, page 50

Quilting Bee Brought Up To This Minute

The invitations to an old-fashioned patchwork quilt party were written on paper blocked off to represent a quilt patch, with some of the squares tinted in water colors to stimulate calico. When the guests arrived they found the chairs draped with quilts and quilts hung at the doors like portieres. The refreshments consisted of small cakes cut in the form of squares, diamonds, hexagons and other shapes employed in quilt making, and were iced in colors similar to the invitations.

For instance, a square cake was decorated in red and white like a nine patch; the hexagon, iced in white, was regularly covered with tiny round chocolate candies in the fashion of a polka dot; some of the cakes were striped. Plaid effects were also easily obtained.

Instead of a tablecloth, square paper doilies tinted like the invitations were used. The centerpiece was a large doll dressed like an old lady, spectacles, cap and all, seated in a miniature rocker and sewing on an old-fashioned quilt. At her side was a basket filled with the favors—small sachets made of satin quilt blocks.

The ice cream was—Neapolitan in stripes of pink and white. The sandwiches were cut in shapes similar to the cakes; some of them of alternate inch-squares of white and brown bread were laid on the plate in the form of a nine-patch.

Among the amusements was a contest to see who could piece the neatest-looking block in five minutes. The woman who did this was awarded the blocks of all the others and all the extra pieces besides, of which—there were enough to make a small quilt.

A laughable affair was the stunt of trying while blindfolded to arrange some cut pieces in their proper pieces to form a block.

L.K.

Springfield Republican
Springfield, Massachusetts
December 12, 1915, page 60

The Story Of Quilts

Antecedents of a Once-Common Domestic Industry

At least two generations are still alive which remember the ample and warm patchwork quilt of their mothers and grandmothers. Indeed, these generations will vividly recall that the winter months generally saw much of the available space of the dining room or "parlor" occupied during parts of the day, at least, by the long, slender quilting frames. Memory will go a step farther and recall the frenzied collection throughout the year of triangular patches of every texture and hue. Somehow that leisurely work on the quilt, once it was stretched on the frames, gave a more homely, if not more congenial, employment to the housewife, her friends and neighbors than does the present-day devotion to bridge.

A first edition of *Marie Webster's Quilts: Their Story and how to make them,* published in 1915 by Doubleday, Page & Company, Garden City, New York. Marie Webster was a successful female entrepreneur, quilt designer and author. She began her career just prior to World War I. Marie's quilt designs were mostly delicate, pastel botanical appliqué quilts. Her popularity rose through the 1930 Depression years. Her home in Marion, Indiana, is an historic landmark dedicated to preserving her contribution to twentieth-century quiltmaking.

It is unlikely that a quiltmaker, or an observer of quiltmaking activity, has ever paused to ask whether this domestic industry has a history or tradition. It may be interesting to them, however, to learn that quiltmaking is a very ancient domestic practice. Marie D. Webster, in "Quilts, Their Story, and How to Make them" (Doubleday, Page: $2.50), tells all about it. The author makes an extended research into the origin and development of the quilt which carries her to a remote point in antiquity. Her discussion of the subject involves considerably more than the mere collection and putting together of the parts of a quilt. She touches also upon the preparation and coloring of the yarns, and the weaving of fabrics. This, of course, comes within the scope of the subject, for quilts broadly speaking, are not in every instance composed of patchwork alone.

The Egyptians, Persians and other eastern folk were, and are, adept at making these fabrics. In most cases, however, these people produce the finished article through use of the loom, rather than by needle and thread and odd bits of cloth.

Their quilts, of the equivalent, often took the form of a tapestry, and comprised most elaborate patterns. They were sometimes woven of silk and sometimes linen, goat wool or cotton, but, in almost every instance, the finished article was a beautiful and highly valuable possession. With the eastern peoples those products were oftentimes employed as hangings, and did duty at other times as couch covers. The Persians had a method of stamping the plain woven fabric with an intricate pattern of leaves, animals, trees, birds and humans, carved on human blocks. These often required the use of several sets before the work was completed. The results were highly artistic. Occasionally these Persians "prints" are to be had at the present time.

Coming down to the 19th century, the quilt, in most cases, was utilitarian, but decorative, notwithstanding. In the housewife's mind utility was generally its chief virtue. At the same time, however, many women of taste and leisure produced exquisite examples of this work—as perfect as mosaics, and wonderful in detail of stitching inlay and harmony of colors. The author has been able to obtain for illustration many striking examples of the finer order of quiltmaking, and several of these are reproduced in detail of color and pattern. The look also contains many illustrated examples of early eastern quiltmaking, but their complicated pattern makes their reproduction in color next to impossible. The origin and development of the quilt as outlined by the author make an interesting story. This amiable bit of research, together with full descriptions of the steps necessary in reproducing original patterns, should be a source of delight to the skilled needlewoman.

Sunbonnet Lassies, a Marie Webster–designed quilt, dated 1912, 41 inches x 52 inches, cotton.
The pattern for this crib size quilt is one of Marie Webster's earliest designs.
Courtesy of the Marie Webster House, Quilters Hall of Fame, Marion, Indiana.

Windblown Tulips, 88 inches x 88 inches, cotton. Marie Webster designed this quilt pattern in 1911. Courtesy of the Marie Webster House, Quilters Hall of Fame, Marion, Indiana.

Plain Dealer
Cleveland, Ohio
January 2, 1916, page 56

Quilting Easy

An easy way to do quilting is to place the lining on the floor perfectly smooth. After the padding and top have been laid on, run lines of long stitches through the quilt about twelve inches apart. Carefully lift it to the sewing machine, letting all the weight rest on chairs to prevent straining the machine needles. Lengthen the stitch on the machine and quilt in lines three inches apart. Cross lines can be run and thus make squares or diamonds if so desired. The work is done more quickly and will last longer than when done by the old method of quilting.

MRS. N.E.K.

Plain Dealer
Cleveland, Ohio
March 14, 1916, page 2

The Halle Bros. Co.

"Album" Quilt—
Made in 1840 and
New Quilting of
1916

The position of honor in the Art Needlework Department is gracefully held this week by an "Album" quilt 76 years old. It is priced at $250.00.

Striking; outside of beauty of color and pattern, is the perfect and dainty state in which the quilt has been kept. Not a stitch is faulty, a rarely exquisite exponent of the stable purpose that characterized the thought as the needle-craft of our great-grandmothers.

Incident to the revival of this old-fashioned handwork, there are new quilting patterns, in prints and in sample color-pattern to show how each block should be laid. The designs are the old floral ones. Thus the aspiring maid who cherishes the memory and zeal of her grandparent, has speedy accurate way of doing the work which was so toilsome long ago.

And in case one should wish it. There are workers busy cutting and basting the designs on the blocks, so that one need do only the fine work of hemming.

In the Wash Goods Section, new quilting ginghams are here, in plain, fast colors, priced at 25c and 50c the yard.

(Second Floor)

Lincoln Daily News
Lincoln, Nebraska
June 10, 1916, page 3

Quilts Have All Passed Out.

Those Our Grandmas Made Are Not Esteemed Now.

In an Indiana village the other day there died an old lady who was known to about the whole community as Grandma Bailey. She was ninety-one years old. When she was about forty, evidently considering herself on the border of old age, according to the custom of a former generation, she started in industriously in the old-fashioned domestic pursuit of making quilts. In the last fifty years of her life, she pieced 2,500 quilts, an average, it will be seen, of about one quilt a week, year in and year out, allowing for an annual vacation of a fortnight.

Presumably, however, Grandma Bailey took no regular vacations, but stuck to her quilt making with great steadiness throughout the year. Of her other achievements in life nothing is recorded, but it is set down in her brief chronicle that she was "a constant reader of the newspapers, and could quote from any chapter in the Bible." In early life she probably had many other activities, but industrially her life work was practically summed up in the record of 2,500 quilts.

The quilt is becoming an obsolete institution, and in many families probably the name even is a strange word. There are modern substitutes in bed coverings that are lighter, warmer and more desirable. The quilt, both in its use and in the method of its construction, is altogether out of harmony with the modern ideas of efficiency. It of hundreds, and sometimes thousands, of small bits of rags, chiefly calico, so cut as to form some symmetry of design, and laboriously sewed together. This was "piecing" the quilt. When the patchwork fabric had grown to sufficient size, a corresponding piece of calico was used for the other side, loose cotton placed between the two, and the whole structure hemmed at the edges and the surfaces threaded or "quilted" at intervals of a foot or so, to bind them together. The quilting was done on a quilting frame, and it was frequently made the occasion of a neighborhood social function ranking in importance and interest with the signing school and the spelling and husking "bees."

Ruby Short (McKim) designed the Quaddy Quiltie bedtime quilt in 1916. It was published in the *Kansas City Star*.

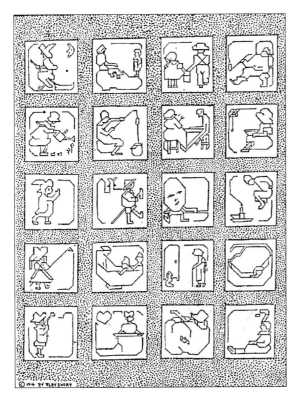

Kansas City Star
Kansas City, Missouri
June 11, 1916, page 10c
No Back Copies of Quilties.
Perhaps Your Friends Have Saved Them.

It will be impossible for back copies of the Quaddy Quilties to be supplied for those of you who have lost yours or who did not save the first ones. However, if you are careful to save all the patterns from this time on, you can make almost as pretty a quilt by embroidering two blocks just alike; say you make two Peter Rabbits and two Mrs. Peter Rabbits. If you don't like that plan you can make a baby comfort with sixteen or twelve quilties. Or maybe you can borrow the missing one from a friend.

As many blocks as you want can be taken from the patterns printed on this page. The way to transfer the Quaddy is to place a piece of carbon or transfer paper over a square of cloth (whatever you are going to use in your quilt). Then put the pattern on this page on top of that and trace its outline on to the cloth.

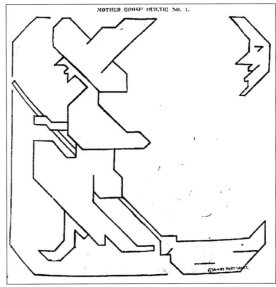

Mother Goose Quiltie, *Kansas City Star*, February 10, 1918, page 11. This quilt is one of the first designed by Ruby Short McKim. Ruby was one another of the emerging twentieth-century quilt designers. Her name and reputation in the world of quiltmaking is legendary.

Mother Goose Quiltie, designed by Ruby Short (McKim) c. 1916, 35 inches x 52 inches, cotton.

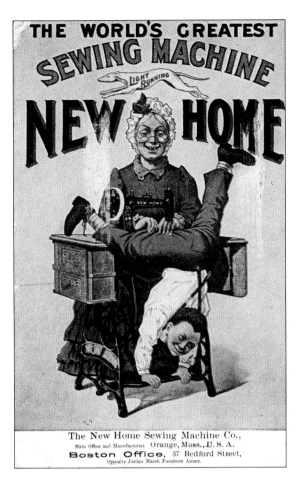

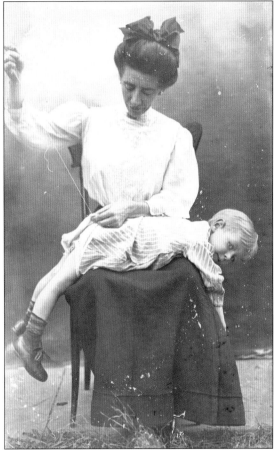

Postcard photo, c. 1915.

Cleveland Gazette
Cleveland, Ohio
July 1, 1916, page 4

Quilt Protector.

Quilt or blanket protectors, stamped for embroidery, cost 35 cents. They are strips of sheer lawn to tack over the end of the quilt or blanket that comes at the head of the bed, in contact with the face. They can be simply hemmed or edged with a narrow valance, fulled on. The patterns for embroidery are simple and can be done in white cotton or in colored cotton to match the stripe in the blanket or the figure in the comforter.

The Stevens Point Journal
Stevens Point, Wisconsin
January 17, 1917, page 1

BOYS HELP MAKE QUILT

Domestic Science Work Reaches Unusual Proportions in Jt. Dist. 9, Amherst, School

Teaching of domestic science is attaining remarkable proportions in the school in Jt. Dist. No. 9, Amherst, of which Miss Viva Phelps is the teacher. The pupils are now engaged in making a large quilt which is to be later disposed of and the proceeds used for the improvement of the school. The boys are interestedly helping in this work as well as the girls.

Miss Phelps has a novel housekeeping system in her school. Each week she appoints a housekeeper and an assistant housekeeper who ap-

Love Chain, c. 1910, 65 inches x 76 inches, cotton. Patriotic red, white and blue in a variation
of Irish Chain design contains the ever popular fabric commonly referred to as Cadet Blue.

Centerfold article featuring quilt patterns of the World War I years.

point other assistants as necessary and look after the care of the school room. The boys offered to assist in the work and are included with the girls in the system which is reported to be working very well. There is a suspicion that Miss Phelps is a practical woman suffragist but no announcements have been made regarding her views.

The proceeds of the recent social at the school have been used to buy a new desk for the teacher. The quilt will be disposed of at another social to be given later.

Miss M.F. McDermott.
New Philadelphia.
Coshocton Morning Tribune
Coshocton, Ohio
February 2, 1917, page 2
Miss Mary Schoonover was very agreeably surprised Monday evening when the members of the Presbyterian Ladies Aid met at her home and presented her with a beautiful blue and white double Irish chain quilt as a birthday present.

Nevada State Journal
Reno, Nevada
February 25, 1917, page 8
The Dorcas Circle of the Baptist church was entertained most delightfully on Tuesday afternoon at the home of Mrs. Rudolf Herz. After the

business session the "blue bird quilt" which had been made by the women of the church, was presented to Mrs. J.B. Wainwright. The quilt netted $122.75 and will be exhibited in the window of the "Gray Shop."

The Washington Post
Washington, D.C.
March 18, 1917, page 23
Mrs. Arthur C. Shaw, president of the Ladies' Auxiliary of De Molay Commandery, No. 4, announces that twelve ladies of the auxiliary are finishing the memory quilt which they started last summer and are now planning for a quilting party. The presentation of the quilt to the Masonic and Eastern Star Home will be something different in the records of fraternal doings. It is stated, and the members of the auxiliary wish every member of the commandery to be represented by the squares which compose the quilt.

The Newark Advocate
Newark, Ohio
March 29, 1917, page 5
Patchwork Quilt Of Silk
One may start a silk patchwork quilt or a cotton one, but the former is easier to make because of the softness of the silk. Scraps cut from old dancing frocks of taffeta or satin in pastel coverings make very dainty quilt.

One charming quilt of this kind was evolved from a cast-off evening coat of pink faille in a delicate morning glory shade and a discarded dance frock of rose-flowered pussy willow taffeta. The pattern was done in blocks, flowered and plain silks cut in triangles and the block joined with strips of pink satin ribbon. Such a quilt should be hued with plain colored thin silk and a sheet of cotton wadding laid between.

"The Correct Display of the Stars and Stripes." The National Geographic, October 1917, page 420. "MAKERS OF THE FLAG. Then conquer we must, when our cause it is just. And this be our motto: "In God is our trust." And the Star Spangled Banner in triumph shall wave. O'er the land of the free and the home of the brave."

The Commerce Journal
Commerce, Texas
August 3, 1917, page 15
Miss Limmie Turley won the blue ribbon on her tobacco sack quilt at the picnic.

Fort Worth Star-Telegram
Fort Worth, Texas
August 31, 1917, page 13
Quilt, Begun in Georgia Before Civil War, Being Finished Here
The election of President Lincoln in 1860 interrupted the making of two quilts, one of which is just now being completed in Fort Worth. Both are remarkable pieces of handiwork and will be prized by their owners not only for their beauty but for their historic associations.

These quilts were started in 1860 by Mrs. P.M. Stratton and her niece, Miss Mary Field of Fayetteville, Fayette county, Georgia. Miss Field then was 18 years old, and it is she, now Mrs. Mary Field Wilson, who is finishing up the last one at the home of her daughter, Mrs. W.C. Harris, Stop 6, Dallas interurban.

Lincoln Wins—War.

Lincoln's election meant but one thing—war. So when it was learned that he had won Mrs. Stratton said:

"Well, Mary, we'll just put these quilts away now. It's no use to finish them, because the Yankees might take them, if they should get down here in Georgia."

So the quilts were put away. Much of the overlaid work, designed to represent a rose cutting, with buds and one flower in full bloom, was placed in Mrs. Stratton's care. Soon after the war Mrs. Stratton went from Georgia to Grimes county, Texas, and later to Galveston. For some time she corresponded with her niece, who had married J.L. Wilson shortly after the war started, but later they lost track of each other. For twenty-five years each believed the other dead.

Located in Cleburne

Finally, some time in the eighties, Mrs. Wilson heard through other relatives that Mrs. Stratton was still living and that she was in Cleburne, Texas. In 1890 Mrs. Wilson moved from Georgia to Ellis county, Texas, and shortly afterward went to Cleburne to visit her aunt. Nothing was said of the quilts at that time, but upon her second visit, Mrs. Stratton asked:

"Mary, do you remember those quilts we started?"

Mrs. Wilson did

"Well, nothing has been done on them since we put them away.

Quilts Given to Mrs. Wilson.

After Mrs. Stratton's death in 1900 the quilts were turned over to Mrs. Wilson and she worked at intervals on them. There were long periods when she could not obtain the desired materials because the cloth was difficult of being matched. One of them has been finished in recent years, however, and was given by Mrs. Wilson to her daughter, Mrs. K.P. Belden of Gainesville. Finishing the second will be delayed unless Mrs. Wilson can find more material to match what she has.

Popular Before the War.

All of the overlaid work is hand-stitched and exceedingly neat. This work, with the bright colors, makes it very pretty. Mrs. Wilson said such fancy quilts were quite popular just before the Civil war.

The second quilt, when finished, will be given to Mrs. Harris.

Mrs. Wilson has vivid recollections of Sherman's march to the sea, his army having passed through Fayetteville. She was away at the time, but declares many homes and a large amount of cotton were burned there. The federal soldiers also took large quantities of food from the Southerners.

Groom Returns to Army.

Mrs. Wilson married during the war. Wilson was one of the early volunteers but was discharged on account of illness at Savannah and they were married soon after he returned. Within a few weeks after they were married Wilson again went into service. He served through the remainder of the war without serious injury. He died about twenty years ago.

Mrs. Wilson now is in her seventy-fifth year, but still is active.

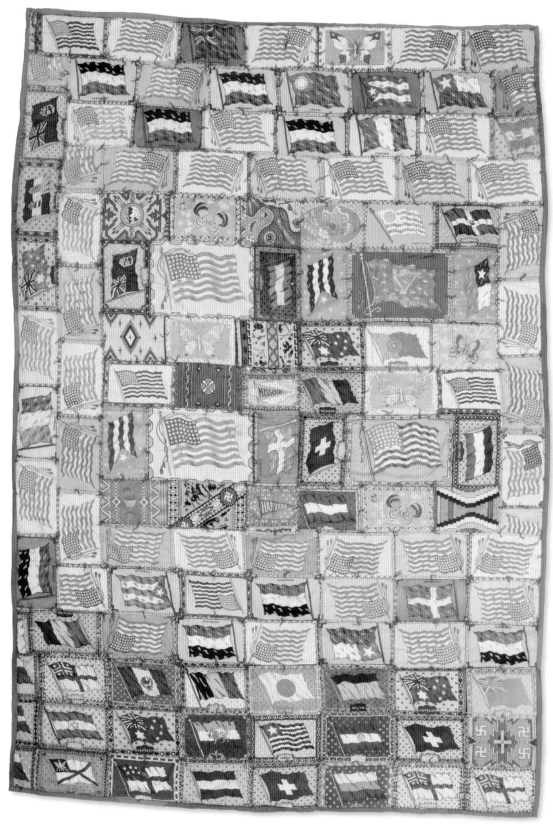

Tobacco Flannel Quilt, c. 1914, 58 inches x 82 inches, cotton flannel. This quilt was pieced with colorful, patriotic flannels originally inserted into the packaging boxes of tobacco in the early twentieth century. The flannels were a peace offering to the wives of the smokers, chewers and dippers of this odiferous herb.

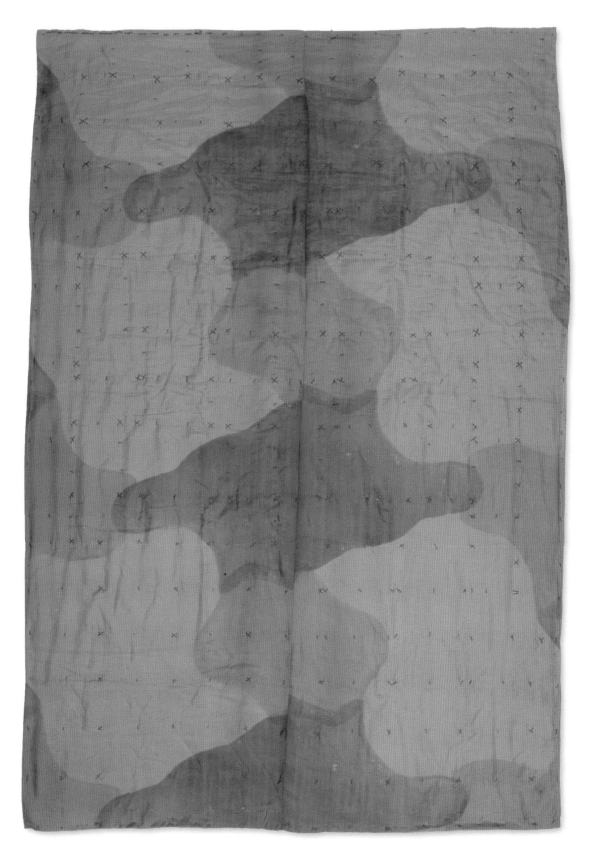

Silk, printed camouflage-style, quilt back.

This Tobacco Flannel is typical of the 1910s. The popular flannels were given away in the sales packaging of men's tobacco. Collecting the flannels was a popular female activity of the time. Many women chose to join them together to create these very time-specific quilts.
Courtesy of The National World War I Museum.

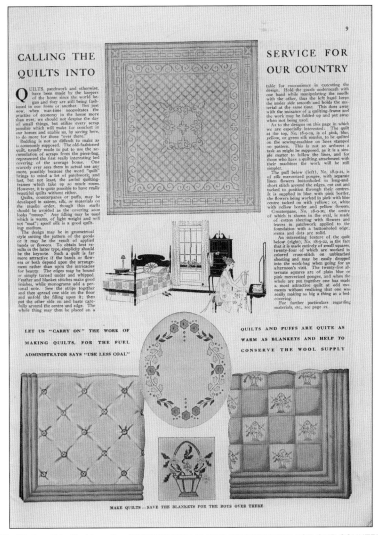

The Modern Priscilla Magazine, "CALLING THE QUILTS INTO SERVICE FOR OUR COUNTRY."
September, 1918, page 9. This fascinating article encourages women to make "Puff quilts" often
called "Biscuit quilts" in order to conserve wool for our soldiers on the battlefront.

Oregonian
Portland, Oregon
November 14, 1917, page 12

**What You Can Make
At Home.
By Mrs. Portland.**

Almost any woman who is at all skillful with hammer, saw and nails can make her own quilting frame —a very necessary piece of furniture if we women are to begin making our own quilts.

A quilting frame consists of two long pieces of board or other lumber—smoothed if possible—and two consid-erably shorter cross pieces. Lengths of left-over moulding or soft wood flooring may be used. The pieces should not be over an inch thick and a few inches wide, so that they can be easily handled. Two long pieces should be about eight feet long and the cross pieces three or four feet long.

When you have sawed your pieces of wood the desired length, the next step is to provide some means of fastening them together temporarily to form the oblong frame on which your quilt is to be stretched for the tacking or quilting together of the upper part and lining. This fastening at the four corners may be accomplished in several ways. You may make little grooves a few inches from the ends of each of the four pieces and then fasten them together with cheap small clamps, which may be screwed and unscrewed as you put in, take out or reroll your quilt or comforter. Or you may, with a large nail or spike, drive holes in each end of the four pieces in such a way that the holes thus made when the nail is pulled out may be used for large screws to hold the frame together.

If you are not adept with nails, screws or hammers, you can bore the holes through your wooden pieces with a stove poker heated red hot. Then your quilting frame can be held together with strings, wire, wooden pegs or nails put through these bored holes. There should be two or three of these holes two or three inches apart at the end of each piece, so you can change the size of your frame if you wish to.

Along the edge of each of the two long pieces tack strips of stout cloth six to eight inches wide and long enough to reach to the holes at each end. When your quilt is ready to put into the frame, its edges are basted or pinned to these strips of cloth and then one side is rolled up until it reaches two or three feet from the other side of the quilt, when the cross pieces are placed on the two ends and fastened firmly. The quilt should be stretched out smoothly and evenly by two persons pulling it from the two opposite sides before the cross pieces are fastened in place. The frame can be set on the backs of four chairs or on small tables or boxes of the proper height. When the first division of the quilt is all tacked or quilted, the cross pieces are removed, another section of the unworked quilt rolled into pieces and the cross pieces again placed in position.

Philadelphia Inquirer
Philadelphia, Pennsylvania
December 7, 1917, page 3
Present Governor with Quilt
Special to The Inquirer.
HOLIDAYSBURG, Pa., Dec. 6.—A bed quilt in the form of a large American shield, with a border of forty-eight stars, will be presented to Governor Martin G. Brumbaugh by the Blair County Teachers' Institute. The quilt is the product of the labors of the pupils of the Fredericksburg public schools, and is on exhibition at the Blair county fruit show. The proposition to buy the quilt for use in the gubernatorial mansion was put before the teachers' institute by former Governor Frank B. Willis, of Ohio, a personal friend of the Pennsylvania Governor.

The Iowa Recorder
Greene, Iowa
December 12, 1917, page 4
The quilt made by the Linger Longer club on which numbers were sold was drawn by Mrs. Geo. Berkley of Allison and netted the club $13 which will be turned into some charitable fund.

The Stevens Point Journal
Stevens Point, Wisconsin
December 22, 1917, page 6
Museum Gets Unique Quilt
Madison—A quilt containing the name and company of every member of the Brodhead, Wis., G.A.R. post was received by the G.A.R. museum in the state capital. The presentation was made by Mrs. Sarah S. Brodhead.

Kansas City Star
Kansas City, Missouri
January 16, 1918, page 7
Made 100 Quilts For Missions.
Indiana Woman, 90 Years Old, Has Done Much for Heathens.
Mrs. Sarah Glossbreuner of Jeffersonville, Md., 90 years old, has just finished the one hundredth patchwork quilt she has made with her own hands and sold in aid of foreign missions.

Crazy Quilt, dated 1918, Arch Street M. E. Church (Methodist Episcopal), 83 inches x 72 inches, silk, velvet, satin.

Inscribed with "Pres W W and Gov M B." Governor Martin Brumbaugh was the governor of Pennsylvania and Woodrow Wilson was the United States President in 1918.

The Coshocton Tribune
Coshocton, Ohio
April 19, 1918, page 6

Cast For The
Entertainment
At Lewisville

Following is the cast of characters for the entertainment of which will be given by the Ladies' Aid society of the Canal Lewisville M.E. church, Friday evening, before the auctioneering of two quilts, "The Wheel of Friendship" and "The Heart Quilt."

Rev. L.D. Spaugy is the only full name inscribed on this quilt, a clue that provided just enough information to get closer to determining where it was made. Rev. L.D. (Lenon) Spaugy can be found in the 1910 census as living in Alliance, Ward 4, Stark County, Ohio, as a minister. By the 1920 census and closer to the World War I years, the Rev. L.D. Spaugy had moved to Tarentum, Ward 1, Allegheny County, Pennsylvania. The only Arch Street M. E. (Methodist Episcopal) Church is located in Philadelphia. So the mystery remains.

State Times Advocate
Baton Rouge, Louisiana
September 19, 1918, page 3
Last Call to the W.C.T.U.

The president of the W.C.T.U., calls attention of the members to the fact that Friday is the regular meeting day of the organization, and reports of the year's work must be made ready for the state convention which will be held in Ruston, in November.

Also, all interested in the making of the quilt, must get together, or their part of this work will be a failure. An urgent appeal is made to all members to be present on Friday afternoon at the Presbyterian annex, promptly at 5 o'clock, to revive interest of the W.C.T.U., in Baton Rouge.

The Newark Advocate
Newark, Ohio
January 13, 1919, page 6
Matter of Patches

Seven-year-old James and his mother were visiting the latter's spinster aunt. As was their custom these maiden ladies showed their visitors

their vast supply of home-pieced quilts. "This is the first four-patch Jane ever made," announced one proudly, displaying a quilt whose blocks were made up of four square pieces.

"And this is Mary's nine-patch," explained Jane. "She made it when she was only seven years old."

The third quilt was an embroidered silk one, made of myriads of tiny irregular pieces—the gifts of friends and the remnants from ancient wedding and reception clothes. James

stared at it a few minutes and then he turned to his mother. "Is this one an all-patch?" he asked.

Philadelphia Inquirer
Philadelphia, Pennsylvania
April 20, 1919, page 2

7536 Patches in Crazy Quilt

POTTSTOWN, Pa., April 19.— Scores of friends of Mrs. Annie Sellers, of Hopewell, are admiring a quilt which she has just completed. The quilt contains 7536 patches and is one of the finest pieces of work ever turn-

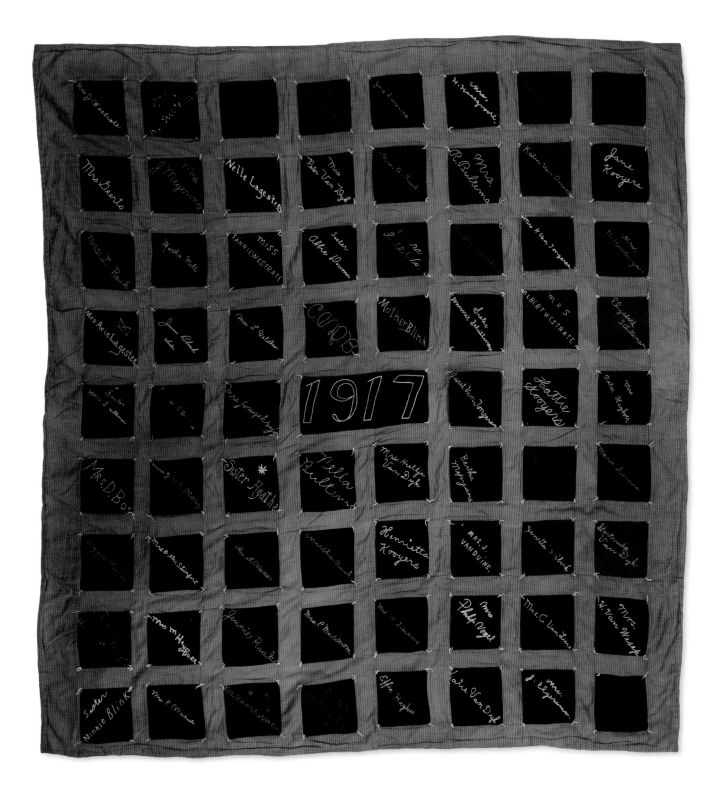

Fund Raising Signature Quilt, Holland, Ottawa County, Michigan, 1917, pieced, hand embroidered, hand tied, wool and cotton.

ed out in the vicinity. She has refused several substantial offers to sell it.

Kansas City Star
Kansas City, Missouri
August 19, 1919, page 11
Quilts From Sugar Sacks.
From the Los Angeles Times.

You know the bags one buys granulated sugar in have the makings of some dainty quilts in them! Get a number of them together, rip and then wash and bleach them in the sun for a day,

Then lay each one out on a table and with a tumbler and lead pencil trace out three intertwining circles. Work these in outline with some delicately colored silk. Of course, you want to work it in the color used in the room upon the bed of which it is to repose in future days.

When you have enough of these pieces worked to make a quilt when joined together, briarstitch them together, quilt and give a border of silk of about a 3 inch depth. You will be pleased with

the result and the only materials you have to buy are the embroidery silk and the border.

Or you might try further patchwork on your sugar bags by the simple addition of some colorful appliqués. Conventional motifs in chambray, calico or challis in strikingly contrasting colors might be posed with wonderfully good effect on sugar bags and treated to a heavy outlining stitch. Which last is invariably striking when it's done with black silk or wool. Try three circles of a vivid orange and purple and green, making them the tumbler size, and "bringing them out" with a black blanket stitched edge. And that is only one of many striking and easy cutout decorations that you can put upon a sugar bags with a patchwork quilt mission in life.

State
Columbia, South Carolina
October 11, 1919, page 6

Just the nicest bundle of quilt scraps came into the office the other

Aunt Sade Brockway Quilt top, c. 1918, hand pieced, 68 inches x 78 inches, cotton.
This quilt top was made with the popular cottons of the 1910s.

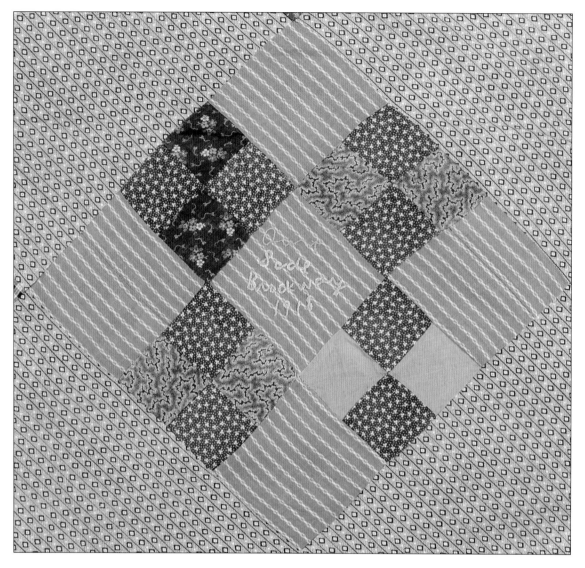

day. All of the difference colors were tied up in separate bundles. We don't mean to brag on ourselves, but we must say that we do have all appreciation of the aesthetic. That bundles of scraps, which was, perhaps, useless to the owner, will mean more than we can say to at least three old ladies. It is going to mean some work that they can do, it will mean extra pocket money to ease things along a little and diversion for the long winter evenings. You would be surprised how hard it is to get scraps. One little old lady needs what the quilt scraps will bring in more than usual, as recently her son, who has T.B., has come to live with her. It helps to make for an independent feeling. Oh, no, we aren't hinting, but of course, if any one was to send in some scraps we wouldn't refuse.

Clotilde newspaper pattern published in the *Oregonian*, Portland, Oregon, February 3, 1918, page 3.

79

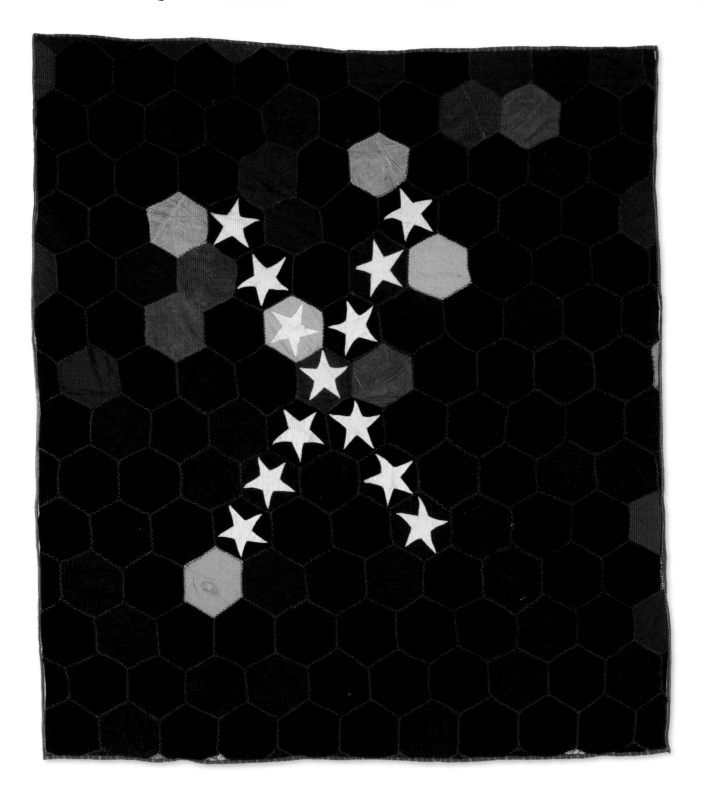

13 Star Hexagon Quilt, c. 1915, 72 inches x 76 inches, cotton or wool. This Hexagon quilt contains an interesting collection of fabrics with all the seams embellished in a feather embroidery stitch. There are 13 stars appliquéd to the top of the quilt.

Postcard, Camp Funston, Fort Riley, Kansas. This military base was reported to be one of the hardest hit by the Spanish Flu. Postmark April 5, 1918.

BEWARE THE FLU

The Latest Victim Sighs
from *Pearson's Weekly*
A splitting head and limbs of lead
A burning throat and dry,
Add to these woes a snuffling nose
A red and streamy eye
Thermometer beneath my tongue
Reads "one-ought-four point two"
Instead of normal "ninety-eight"
I've got the Spanish "flu."[5]

Both life and quiltmaking were interrupted in 1918–1919, and World War I was only partly to blame. A pandemic influenza virus now known as H1N1 swept the world killing 50 to 100 million or 3 to 5 percent of the world's population.[6] This virulent illness was selective, striking disproportionately at young adults, ages 20 to 40

years, usually the healthiest members of society. World War I with its massive troop concentrations contributed to rapidity of transmission. "The Flu," sometimes referred to as "the Spanish Flu," did not discriminate for nationality. From the frozen tundra of Alaska to the tropical-paradise islands of the South Pacific, the Flu ravaged entire villages until its end in 1919. Philadelphia, Baltimore, and Washington D.C. were the hardest hit cities in the United States.

Gathering in public places was banned as were public funerals even in the outdoors on church lawns. "Masks provided by the Red Cross were encouraged for use in congested gatherings. A half teaspoonful of salt in a glass of water may be used as a spray for the throat and nose was suggested as a preventative.[7] In a few short months, the influenza death toll claimed a much heavier toll of American life than that of the Great War.[8] The following letter from a health care worker underscores this deadly epidemic.

Tales of Fighting Flu
October 24, 1918
Dear Friend Herb,

I just received your letter today and was mighty glad to hear from you. I didn't know what could be the trouble that you hadn't answered my letter. I am, however, glad to hear that you are getting along as good as you are, following your operation.

I have been in good health ever since I left home, but say, Herb, I certainly had quite a job to take care of here for about three weeks. When the Spanish influenza became so bad, they opened a number of emergency hospitals here and appointed me as wardmaster. I get along just fine, but it certainly does keep me busy all of the time. At the present, the epidemic situation is much better here.

We lost about 732 men in the three weeks, but I was lucky, I didn't have one pass away in the ward which I had charge of. They took in 1,100 patients a day. This sounds like a large number, but it is just the way they were sending them to the hospital. They would admit the patients in the emergency hospitals and if the officers would find that they were in a serious condition, they would at once transfer them to the main hospital.

I had the 219 patients and about twenty men doing the work, as you can imagine how busy I was. It would be hard to explain everything in a letter because it would take quite a long time. Maybe I will get a chance to tell you some day. They have closed all the emergency hospitals now, and I am now in the major's office. His name is Alexander.

Herman A. Lindenburg
"Medical Detachment, Base Hospital,
Camp Zachary Taylor, Ky."[9]

Bellingham Herald
Bellingham, Washington
December 7, 1918, page 6
FOREST GROVE, Dec. 7—The Forest Grove auxiliary of the Bellingham Red Cross met at the home of Mrs. Harry Guckert on November 30 and decided not to hold the fall festival as previously announced, but to send all contributions to the Superfluity shop in Bellingham, where they will be sold for the benefit of the Red Cross. Mrs. Arthur McMillan held the lucky number that drew the Red cross quilt. The local Red Cross will not meet again until after the holidays on account of the prevalence of influenza.

Morning Star
Rockford, Illinois
May 30, 1919, page 4
Vicinity News
OAK GROVE
The secretary of the Red Cross, Mrs. M.P. Scriber submitted the following report of work done during that time which was greatly hindered last fall during the flu epidemic when no meetings were held: pieced quilt and 1 bed quilt finished; 48 bed shirts; 24 pajamas sets; 43 garments; 10 child undershirts; 10 men's drawers; 102 prs socks darned; 10 womens' skirts; 50 handkerchiefs hemmed; 20 infant dresses; 20 infant jackets; 10 infant shirts; 20 child dresses; making 233 garments made. October 24, there was a donation to the emergency hospitals during the epidemic.

In order to stem the tide of contagion, the United States government took Herculean steps to inform the public about the Flu, its symptoms and preventative measures. It urged "It is a patriotic duty to keep well. All sick persons add to the country's burdens. Everybody should be on guard against 'flu' and become thoroughly familiar with symptoms and precautionary measures." Bacteriologists of the time identified the offending germ as Pfeiffer's bacillus.[10] For the sickest of the sick, the disease progressed to pneumonia. The associated cough and sneezing spread the Flu in very small droplets of expelled mucus. Great care was encouraged

Gammy Elder Sampler, Potholder Quilt made by Harriet Eva St. Clair Strong Elder, Providence, Rhode Island. 81 inches x 76 inches, cotton. This quilt was made by Harriet affectionately known by her family as Gammy Elder. She presented the quilt as a wedding gift to her son, Leroy Vincent Elder and his bride, Esther Grace Hershey in 1915. Esther died in 1918 from the Spanish Flu while nursing World War I soldiers back to health in the Boston area. Courtesy of Polly Mello.

Sara Baughman's Hap, c. 1916, hand pieced, hand embroidered, 88 inches x 98 inches, wool. Sara Baughman was age 16 in 1916 when she made this wool Crazy quilt often referred to as a "hap" in Pennsylvania. Sara was living with her parents, Charles and Febie, in Tyrone, Perry County. Sara's father farmed their land on Kennedy Valley Road. Take note of the whisker cloth applied to the top edge of the quilt.

in the treatment of these secretions. Uncle Sam provided advice for the care of the sick room after recovery or death. Bed clothes and any cloth items were to be gathered up and burned.[11]

Cotton bed quilts are the most acceptable for use on the sick bed. Cotton textiles can successfully be sterilized through bleaching and boiling. Silk, velvet and wool quilts would be totally impractical to comfort the ill. It is likely thousands of bed quilts were destroyed between 1918 and 1919 to curb the spread of the awful pandemic Flu.

Kalamazoo Gazette
Kalamazoo, Michigan

October 29, 1918, page 4
Warning!

Don't ride in crowded street cars,
It is altogether wrong;
Just wait upon the corner
Till an empty comes along.
Or, maybe it were better if
You buy a runabout,
For the Spanish flu will get you—
If you don't watch out!
To cough or sneeze in public
Is an act that's not allowed;
You mustn't cast a shadow
For a couple is a crowd.
Avoid all crowded places
For beyond a bit of doubt,
The Spanish flu will get you—
If you don't watch out!

Sara Baughman's Leap Year Hap, dated 1916, hand pieced, hand embroidered, 88 inches x 97 inches, wool. Sara made these two similar quilts in 1916 perhaps for her impending marriage. Both quilts have whiskers cloths applied to their top edges to protect from heavy abrading from the facial hair of a future husband. Oddly Sara incorporates World War I era tobacco flannels providing a patriotic touch.

The condition of both quilts is as pristine as the day they were made. One can only speculate that Sara's life might have been cut short by the Spanish Flu. (The Flu selectively killed more young people ages 20-40 years of age.) Perhaps her parents kept the quilts to honor the memory of their lost daughter or perhaps it is possible Sara's intended was called into the service of his country and sadly did not return from the horrors of war.

Church Yard Quilt, c. 1915, 90 inches x 71 inches, wool. Courtesy of Polly Mello.

2. LOYAL TO THE CAUSE: QUILTS FOR SOLDIERS

Throughout our nation's history and especially in a time of war, Americans have always rallied around their soldiers and troops with unbounded generosity and support. This was certainly true during World War I. When the call went out in the fall of 1917 from President Woodrow Wilson for support of our military and benevolent institutions such as the Red Cross, the generations from our youth to the elderly met the call.

Children, wives, mothers and grandchildren used their needlework skills to aid the men of their families on the battlefront. Knitting was the most popular form of needlework assistance, however, women also applied their quiltmaking to commemorative and fundraising quilts during our country's eighteen month involvement in World War I.

The following article clearly represents the American spirit on the homefront in a time of war. It appeared on May 15, 1919 on page 2 of *The Ann Arbor News*, Ann Arbor, Michigan.

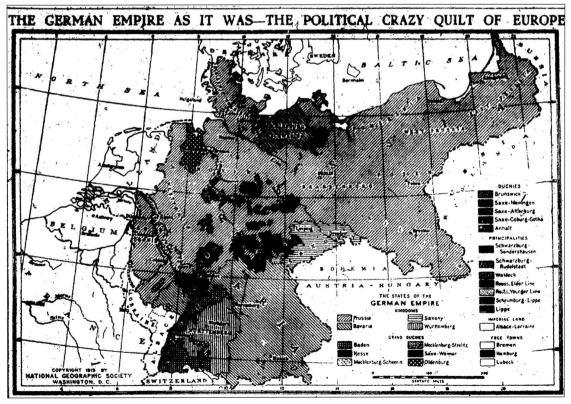

San Antonio Light, San Antonio, Texas, November 6, 1918, page 11. "This German empire resembled nothing to much as a political crazy quilt with patches of varying sizes and shapes belonging to kingdoms, grand duchies, principalities, duchies, etc."

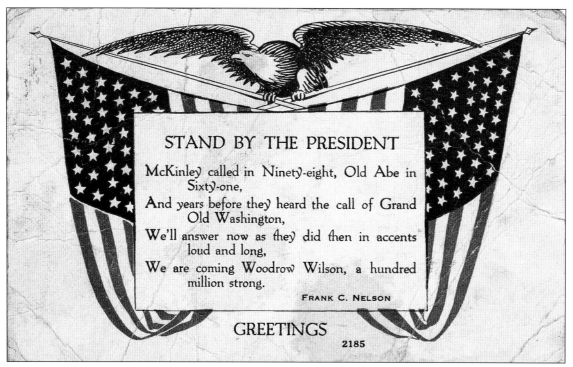

Postcard postmarked 1919.

Women Backing The Soldier Boys

When the history of the war has been written the work done by the women at home will impress itself upon this nation as few even now realize. Literally, millions of women left their homes and took up war activities into which women had never before been called, and many more at home devoted long hours at work in knitting and preparing surgical dressings for the boys "over there."

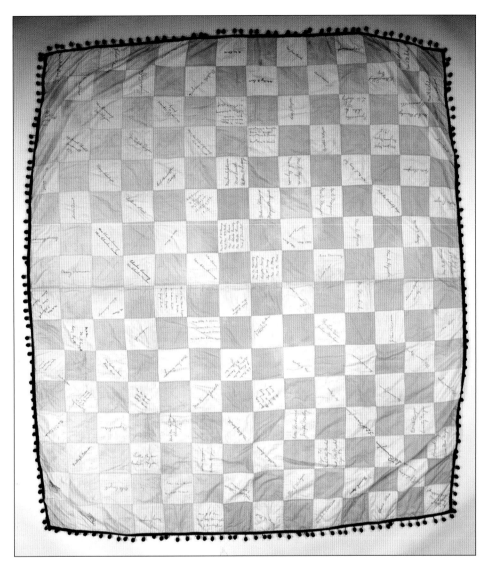

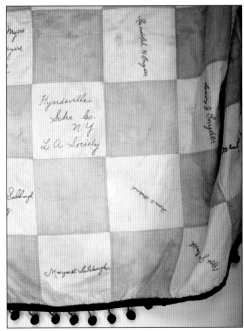

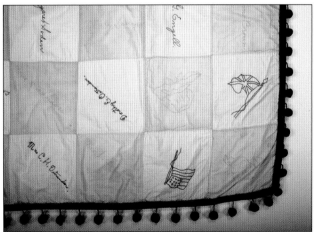

Embroidered Fund Raising Quilt, dated 1912, signed "L. A. Society" (Ladies Aid), Hyndsville, Schoharie County, New York. In one corner, the American Flag and the Union Jack are featured.

Cigar Silk Quilt, c. 1917, 22 inches x 26 inches, silk. The center of this small piece features the flags of the Allied nations in World War I.

You answered the call to the colors,
You proved you were loyal and true;
And we-who can't go-will let others know
The debt that we all owe to you!

Crazy Quilt, dated 1918, 64 inches x 64 inches, silk. The date, the poppy and an
American flag all contribute to making this a very ornate World War I quilt.

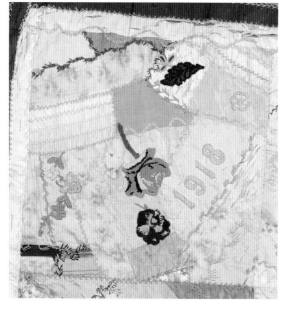

Jackson Citizen Patriot
Jackson, Michigan
May 6, 1918, page 8

"Patriotism is an emotion that grows by sacrifice," says a writer in the Literary Digest. "It is not until we know its cost that we realize our love of country. So women must make their sacrifice first, and having given up to the country the men they love, find that they are the country. For nations are people, not the land on which they live."

Maltese Cross, signed Xmas, 1918, 81 inches x 81 inches, wool. This multitudinous pieced quilt was constructed with 1125 pieces.

Flag woven and made up by millworkers at Manchester, New Hampshire. *The National Geographic Magazine,* October 1917, page 411.

Ad, Leslie's Weekly, May 18, 1918, page 707.

"GIRL SPENDS TWO YEARS IN MAKING QUILT TO BE SOLD FOR BENEFIT OF THE RED CROSS," *Denver Post,* Denver, Colorado, April 14, 1918, page 19. "A young Denver miss, and the quilt which she made which will be sold for the benefit of the Red Cross. She is the daughter of Mr. and Mrs. Byron Tallman, 4214 Pecos street, and worked for two years on the quilt, which she made from pieces of her dresses since she was a little girl. There are 840 pieces of silk and satin in the quilt. which measures eight feet square. The members of Queen City Homestead No. 69, Brotherhood of American Yeoman, will have charge of the selling of the quilt. Inserted is a picture of Miss Tallman's brother, William A. Tallman, who is now serving with the United States navy in European waters."

The Sheboygan Daily Press
Sheboygan, Wisconsin
December 12, 1910, page 8

The ladies of the G.A.R. of this city have sent a beautiful hand made quilt to the Sons of Veterans Home in Mason City, Iowa, for a Christmas gift. The quilt is in block figure and each block contains 20 names worked in red, white and blue. It represents many days of hard work and will undoubtedly be appreciated.

Aberdeen Daily News
Aberdeen, South Dakota
December 22, 1910, page 3

W.R.C. Social

*Patriotic Social Was Very Pleasant
and Well Attended Affair*

The Women's Relief Corps gave a red, white and blue social on Tuesday evening and the contest for the handsome quilt in the national colors came to a close. Mrs. Margaret F. Gardner winning the prize. Mrs. Gardner had 463 votes and Mrs. Matton over 200. The hall and tables were beautifully decorated with red, white and blue, and a delicious supper was served. Games were played and all had a very good time. Over $80 was raised to repay the women for their work with the quilt and the affair was a most successful one in every way.

Plain Dealer
Cleveland, Ohio
May 23, 1911, page 8

Plenty of Quilts for Butts

ATLANTA, Ga., May 22.—When Capt. Archie Butt, military aid to President Taft, inserted an advertisement for an old-fashioned Georgian quilt, he did not think that he would have submitted for his inspection more than 278 of them. The prices asked for the quilts are from $25 up to $125. It is said that Capt. Butt wants the quilt to adorn a bridal bed.

Times-Picayune
New Orleans, Louisiana
May 23, 1911, page 1

**Major Archie Butts Falls To Cupid;
Gets Old-Time Quilt For Chamber.**

Atlanta, Ga., May 22—Old-fashioned

Georgia quilts of every imaginable color and design, from the quiet-hued and somber to the gay and gaudy— just 278 of them in number—poured into the office of Attorney Albert Howell to-day in response to his published request for a Georgia quilt competition that he could select one for his warm friend, Major Archibald W. Butt, aide to President Taft, who desired it as an appropriate feature of the decorations of his new Washington home.

Rumor has it persistently that Major Butt is contemplating a life partner and that his furnishing of a new home is in preparation for that great event. At any rate, he wrote to his friend, Albert Howell, that one thing he needed and desired was an old-fashioned Georgia quilt. A little newspaper story expressing this desire did the rest.

Quilts poured upon Mr. Howell to-day from all over the state. Competition was keen and the makers wanted to wait right there until the thing was decided. They were finally induced to leave their quilts and addresses and a committee went to work on them this afternoon. When the committee started in Mr. Howell's law office looked like the quilt department of a Georgia state fair.

Wilkes-Barre Times-Leader
Wilkes-Barre, Pennsylvania
February 4, 1913, page 10

5982 Piece Quilt
Made By Veteran, 80
Sent To President

WASHINGTON, FEB. 4.—President Taft was today the recipient of a quilt containing 5982 red, white and blue triangles, the handiwork of F. R. Reid, aged 80, of Marlena, Neb., a civil war veteran.

Tobacco Flannel Quilt, c. 1913, 58 inches x 51 inches, cotton. World War I era,
ship pennants are appliquéd around the border of the quilt.

Notice, *The Washington Post*, Washington, D.C., September 29, 1915, page 7.

THE EARTHQUAKE—By Arthur Train

KEWPIE GOES TO WAR

Rose Cecil O'Neill Wilson,
Fort Wayne Weekly Sentinel,
Fort Wayne, Indiana, April 24,
1915, page 6.

"Kewpie is an elf but he gives one the flesh and blood feeling. There is a strange co-mingling of poetry, fantasy, humor, human feeling and subtle psychology in this creation of the gifted woman artist, author and dreamer."[12]

By 1913, Rosie O'Neill, age 31, was "one of the richest, cleverest, and most famous writers and artists in America."[13] Twelve years earlier, Rosie sold the family cow to obtain enough money to journey to New York City with her drawings and manuscripts. Born in Wilkes Barre,

Pennsylvania, she grew up on the Nebraska prairie. She never attended art school or had a single drawing class but she was already writing novels and illustrating periodicals when her large family moved to the Ozarks. Bonniebrook was the family's new home surrounded by babbling brooks, giant sycamores, the fragrance of honeysuckle vines, and the mountain people of Missouri. In her "studio in the treetops,"[14] Rosie refined her writing and drawings talents: "When a child of my brain is clamoring to be born I come up here and work until it is born."[15]

THE BIRTH OF KEWPIE

As an illustrator for *Ladies' Home Journal,* Rosie enhanced her love stories with cupids she dubbed *Kewpies* (baby talk for "cupids"). The rest of the world quickly fell in love with her angelic creations with the turnip top hair. An expert marketer, Rose aligned herself with *Woman's Home Companion* and The Royal Society of Embroidery to publish "pre-stamped dresser scarfs, bibs, fancy bags, and other novelties."[16] An Embroidery Society ad stated "Every one concedes these Kewpies to be the cutest, most lovable little creatures ever made to make people smile." The Society advertised in the *Trenton Evening Times*, Trenton, New Jersey, on September 2, 1913, with: "Kewpies are now sold in Royal Society Package outfits some stamped and tinted on fine white lawn for satin stitch and outline embroidery others are stamped on white huck for darning and outline embroidery."

Rosie also worked closely with German doll manufacturer George Borgfeldt and the dollmakers of the Thuringian Forest, insisting that "This Kewpie doll is to carry a smile to the world and must be sweet and funny."[17] The *Colorado Springs Gazette* reported in 1913 the popularity of Kewpies over "all corners of the world from New Zealand to Timbuctoo."[18] Even new mothers would style their infants' hair to imitate the Kewpie curl. In the United States, the Kewpie Dolls made of bisque, celluloid, and rubber were billed as "the quaintest, queerest, and most lovable little creatures the Doll Family has ever before seen. An odd little body, with the cutest, cunning smile, and queer out-stretched hands and fingers. To look upon them is to put one in good humor and a laughable, jolly mood; you just cannot resist the smile."[19] Made in sizes from one inch to three feet in height, Rosie's beloved, impish Kewpie became the best selling doll in history to that date.[20]

In 1921, Rosie broke her own pledge that no man would enter Bonniebrook, her beloved mountain retreat and the birthplace of Kewpie, when she wed her third husband, Capt. Jean Gallenne, a French World War I veteran.[21]

Salt Lake Telegram
Salt Lake City, Utah
November 23, 1916, page 6

Mabey's Home Made
Quilt Is Missing;
G.O.P. Women Quiet
(By *The Telegram*'s Serial News Series.)

LAYTON, Nov. 23.—What became of a certain quilt made by the woman of Layton will be one of the mooted questions of Utah history. Prominent Republican women etched their names into a quilt at campaign time which was to be presented to C.R. Mabey, when he took up his abode in Washington. It is said that the quilt has disappeared and that no woman in town admits ever having known anything about it.

Aberdeen Daily News
Aberdeen, South Dakota
April 12, 1917, page 4

Company "L" Boys Need
More Blankets
Aberdeen People Are Asked
To Donate Either Quilts
Or Blankets

When you got home from the show last night and noticed the weather was getting slightly chilly you probably took down an extra quilt or blanket from the closet shelf and thought nothing mere of it.

But it's sadly different with the boys of Company L, while they are camping outside. When they noticed that the wind was getting sharp they in all probability resigned themselves to fate and walked around all night or shivered in their bunks on the ground. No—they didn't put their overcoats on—they've had them on all the time.

Today Max Stokes has asked for fifty quilts or blankets to be sent immediately to the Aberdeen boys who are guarding the public and freezing at the same time.

Anyone wishing to donate a quilt or blanket to this worthy cause is

Kewpie Redwork Quilt, c. 1914, designed by Rosie O'Neill, 82 inches x 72 inches, cotton.

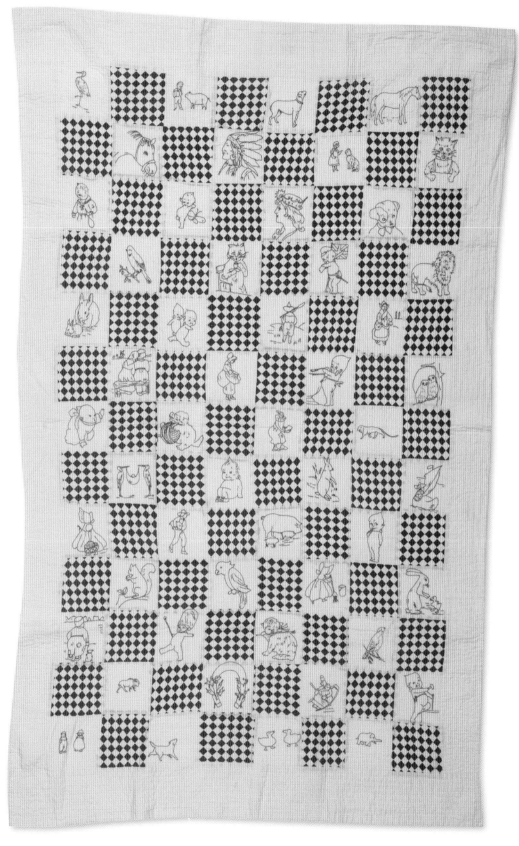

Redwork Quilt, c. 1914, 40 inches x 58 inches. This Redwork quilt features a doughboy
holding the Union Jack. The alternative checkerboard block is pre-printed patchwork.

asked to notify Lieutenant Stokes—
or, better than that—bring it down
with you in the morning to the office
in the Citizens bank building. Aberdeen people should do everything
possible to make the boys comfortable.

Oregonian
Portland, Oregon
June 12, 1917, page 11
**Twelve-Year-Old Girl Doing
Her Bit for her Country.**
*Quilt Being Made to Keep a Sol-
dier Warm—Patriotism Begets
Verse.*

The grown-ups are not the only patriots. Not even if they are buy-
ing liberty bonds and working for the
Red Cross. There are many little children in Portland who are getting the
spirit of service and sacrifice and are
setting a good example to their elders.

One little schoolgirl, who has just
celebrated her 12th birthday, is dem-
onstrating that even a little maid can
do her bit and do it with the right
spirit. Every spare moment is devoted
by the child to knitting squares that
will be joined together and made up
into a wonderfully gay and warm and
comfortable quilt for the soldier boys.

In a letter to a relative this little
maid wrote: "You see, I am patriotic
and am getting to be a 'poetress,' too.
To show that I am patriotic, here is
one of them." That was the way she
put it and here is the verse she wrote:

My Bit.
I am crocheting some crazy "squares"
Instead of selling old tin wares!
I make them for the soldiers brave,
About whom I always rave.
They are made of every hue,
Pink and yellow, green and blue.
They are very soft and warm,
And shield the men from every storm.
They are of "varies" sizes,
And never would win prizes,
But in spite of their shape and hue,
I have done my bit for the Red, White and
Blue.

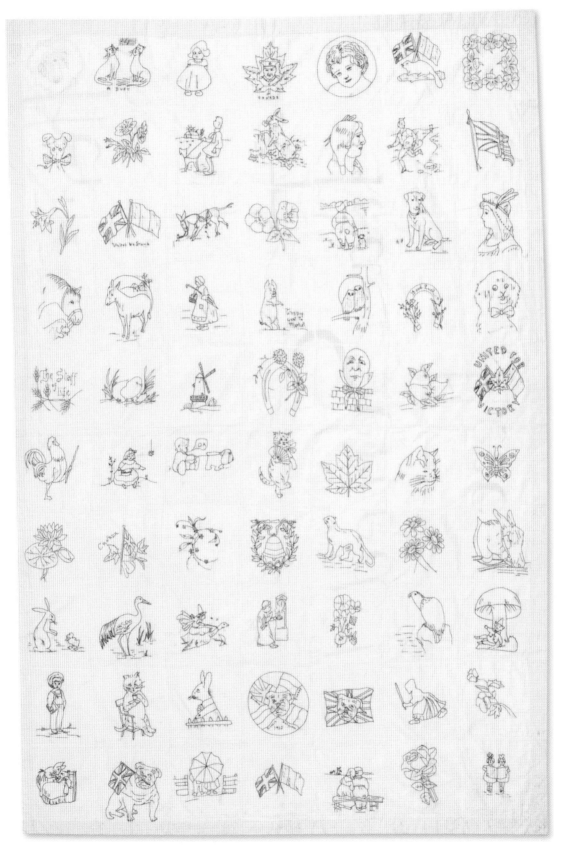

World War I Canadian Redwork Quilt, dated 1915, hand embroidered, 82 inches x 54 inches, cotton. This Canadian quilt is embroidered with images indicating it was made during the war. It may be one of the earliest Victory quilts.

New Castle News
New Castle, Pennsylvania
July 17, 1917, page 10
New Flag Shows That
Boy Is serving U.S.
Peculiar Looking Emblem Floated
On East North Street Has Arous-
ed Some Curiosity.

Peculiar appearance of a flag that
has been unfurled in front of a home-
on East North street has created some
comment. An inquiry shows that it
is a flag which is being used
throughout the country designating
the fact that a son in the family is
fighting for Uncle Sam.

The flag is at the residence of D.
J. Davis, 212 East North street. It
is about 4 feet long and three feet
wide, being a panel of white on a
red flag, with a blue star on the
white panel.

The flag is a home made emblem.

Aberdeen Daily News
Aberdeen, South Dakota
April 13, 1917, page 6
Bundle Contained
Blanket and Quilt
For Co. "L" Boys

"Who was that man with the terri-
bly large bundle who went down the
street this morning and turned in at
the Citizens bank building?"

"It must certainly have been something very important or he never
would have carried it down with him
so early in the morning."

Such remarks and questions were
heard on all hands today. Looking up
the matter it was found that the bundle was "large" and the matter was
"very important."

The man was taking "that old crazy
quilt and the heavy blanket that have
been around the house for so long"
down to Lieutenant Max Stokes to
be sent to the boys of Company L.
Several quilts and blankets have been
brought in but there are still many
more needed.

Any quilts or blankets that are do
nated now will be greatly appreciated
by the members of the company but
its now—not in July or August—that
they are needed.

Oregonian
Portland, Oregon
November 10, 1917, page 12
What You Can Make
At Home
By Mrs. Portland

To help make things look more
Christmassy for your soldier laddie, or some other soldier laddie whom
you want to have come and spend a
part of the Yuletide with you, why not
make a Star of Bethlehem quilt or bed-
spread? Such a quilt being one in
which the Christmas colors, green and
red, predominate, with enough neutral
coloring to give a good background.

An eight-pointed star is easiest made.
For this cut one large square of red
4x4 inches and four squares in neutral
colors, 2x2 inches; also four red squares
2x2 inches. Cut the red squares in two
diagonally to make eight half squares.
Sew these eight half squares to the
large red square, two to each side with
their diagonal sides toward each other
and middle of that side. When this
is done, you will have a regular eight-

Redwork World War I Sampler Quilt, dated 1915, Canada. The images on this quilt include the
Canadian flag, the Union Jack, the Maple Leaf and Soldier. This is an early Victory quilt.

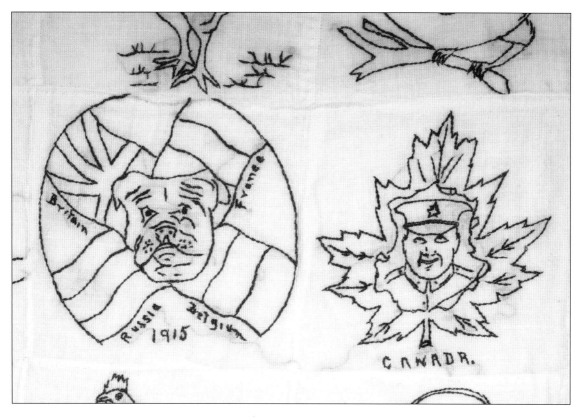

Although this c. 1918 Blue Star Honor Roll Quilt is worn and torn, it features the names of men who served in World War I from Harveyville, Kansas. Courtesy of the National World War I Museum.

Close-up of Blue Star Honor Roll Quilt. Courtesy of the National World War I Museum.

pointed star of red. Sew the four neutral colored squares into the four corners and cut half squares in the neutral color to fit the four empty spaces remaining. When your block is completed, it will be about eight inches square. Set the blocks together with squares of green or oblong pieces, 4x8 inches. This will give you a quilt in which green is the predominating color for background with red stars brought out by their edgings of neutral colors.

Or you can have but the two colors, green and red in the quilt, by making the corner squares and side half squares of green instead of some other colors. Green and red are not usually good colors in cotton, as they are apt to fade and run and streak in washing, so such a quilt as this would be better made in woolen or silk goods than in cotton. The best pieces of discarded red waists, house dresses, linings, etc., may be used, while an old green dress or wrap or the cuttings left from such garments may afford enough pieces for the green part.

If you want to add a little more bright color to the quilt when you fasten the top and lining together you can use silver or gold-colored cord or yarn for knotting, placing it at regular intervals in the stars or the green background.

Crocheted pictorial World War I soldiers with the American flag and the Star Spangled Banner are worked into the coverlet.
(Photographed on a burgundy background to enhance the image.) Courtesy of Laura Fisher Quilts.

Fort Worth Star–Telegram
Fort Worth, Texas
December 21, 1917, page 14
OLNEY RED CROSS
SENDS 162 COMFORTS

The Red Cross at Olney has sent 162 quilts, comforts and pillows to Camp Bowie. Several of the quilts were made in the Red Cross rooms at Olney.

The Stevens Point Journal
Stevens Point, Wisconsin
December 22, 1917, page 6
Museum Gets Unique Quilt

Madison—A quilt containing the name and company of every member of the Brodhead, Wis., G.A.R. post was received by the G.A.R. museum in the state capital. The presentation was made by Mrs. Sarah S. Brodhead.

This pillow cover showcases the Blue Star Service flag. The flag was designed in 1917 by Army Captain Robert Queisser in honor of his two sons serving in World War I. It indicates that one has a loved one deployed and the hope that he/she be returned home safely. After the war, President Wilson designated the Blue Star Mothers an official national organization.

Ad, *Clearfield Progress,* Clearfield, Pennsylvania, June 25, 1918, page 2.

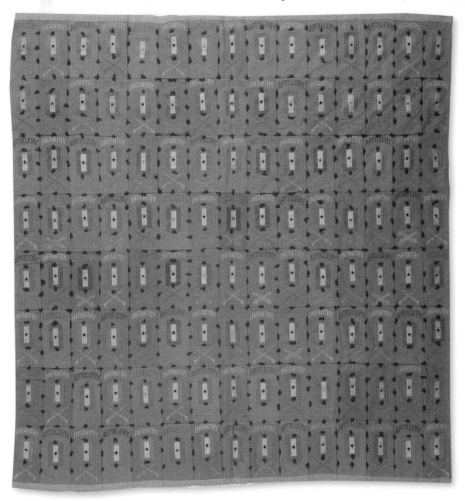

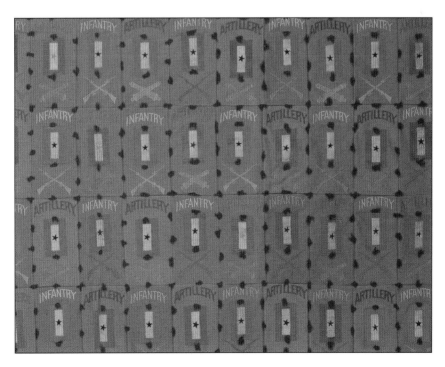

World War I Service Flag Quilt, 72 inches x 70 inches, wool. The embroideries of Blue Star Service flags, Artillery, Infantry and their symbols on this quilt were all accomplished on industrial strength embroidery machines.

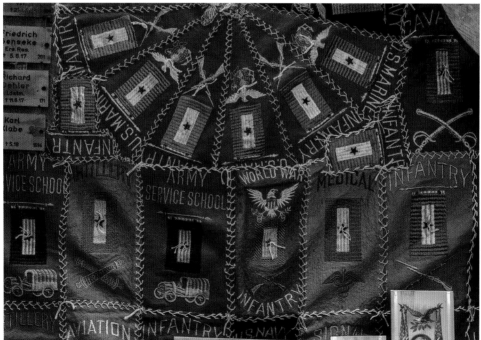

These two photos are of the Service Flag Quilt permanently on exhibit at The National World War I Museum in Kansas City, Missouri. Courtesy of The National World War I Museum.

Service Flag Quilt, c. 1918, wool. This outstanding quilt combines Blue Star Service flags with patriotic slogans and symbols of World War I. Courtesy of the Des Plaines History Center, Des Plaines, Illinois, 1976.318b, WWI quilt.

Cigar Silk Quilt, c. 1915, 71 inches x 91 inches, silk and cotton. This quilt has hundreds of images of famous people from the early twentieth century, national flags, and other war-related motifs. Most likely it was made in Great Britain.

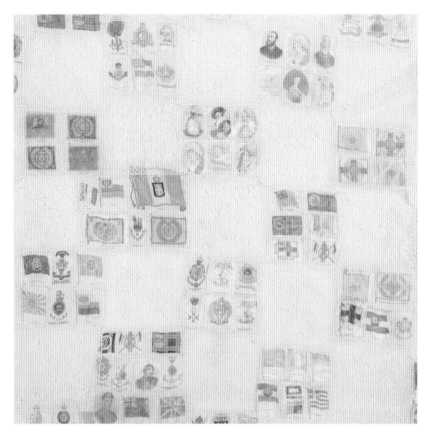

Columbus Ledger
Columbus, Georgia
January 13, 1918, page 6
Ladies of W.C.T.U.
Send Soldiers Quilt

The ladies of the local W.C.T.U. will send a quilt to the soldier boys at Camp Wheeler on Monday which was made of samples of woolen goods donated by Philip Haskell and H. Geyer. The quilt is not only an attractive one but it will be source of great comfort to some of the boys during the cold weather.

Jonesboro Daily Tribune
Jonesboro, Arkansas
July 17, 1918, page 4
Governor Brough Contributes to Quilt

Little Rock, July 17.—Governor Brough yesterday contributed to the Pershing Quilt which is to be presented to Gen. Pershing with the request that he allow the proceeds from the contributions to be used by the convalescent patients among our soldier boys in France. Every governor in the Union has been asked to take a square in the quilt, giving his state and the state he represents. President Wilson, ex-President Taft, ex-President Roosevelt, and Mrs. Gresham Dodd, the first American mother to sacrifice her boy in the European war, will have their names embroidered on the quilt.

Evansville Courier and Press
Evansville, Indiana
July 24, 1918, page 4
Names Of Service Men
Are Shown On Quilt

MT. CARMEL, Ill., July 23.—(Special)—The ladies of the Methodist church at Friendsville have completed a Red Cross quilt which contains the names of the boys of Wabash county who are in the service of their country. The quilt contains 360 names. It will be offered for sale and the ladies ex-pect to realize several hundred dollars from it.

Morning Olympian
Olympia, Washington
August 15, 1918, page 1
Community Workers Are
Busy Making Quilts
Aiding Recreational Commit-
Tee In Getting Ready For
Winter Time.

When community workers will bring sewing machines on wheelbarrows and tote quilting frames on their shoulders, it is taken to mean business. Just so is the interest Roosevelt community helpers took this week in adding more quilts for the winter supply at the soldier and sailor dormitories.

Twenty-three quilts were finished at the Roosevelt school Tuesday at an all-day session, with luncheon at the building at noon. Twenty-eight women worked. This brings the total up to more than 50 quilts since Mrs. Daniel Setchfield resumed the work this summer for the Olympia recreational committee. Mrs. Setchfield has had charge of the quilt furnishing job since last winter, when approximately 100 were made.

The major portion of the heavy and light blankets which were loaned for use by the state highway commission last summer, were recalled for the coming winter, but the response of the various communities throughout the county will replenish the needed supply. Outside of community work much individual quilt work has also been done. Practically all of the lining and cotton is purchased by the recreational committee, while the pieces and work is donated by the workers.

Redwork Victory Quilt, c.1918, 80 inches x 76 inches, cotton. The bell with "Welcome Home" and "Victory" makes this quilt an early example of a Victory quilt.

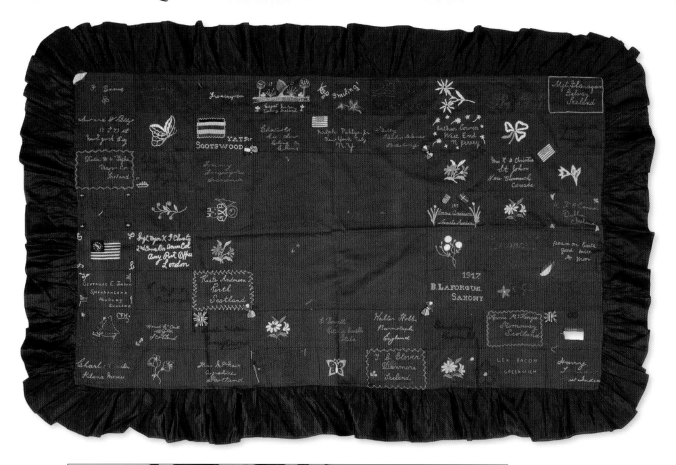

World War I Signature Quilt, dated 1917, 65 inches x 42 inches, cotton. This quilt was inscribed with names of soldiers and people from the Allied countries of World War I.

New Castle News
New Castle, Pennsylvania
August 22, 1918, page 4

The Service Flag

Under the terms of a bill introduced in the lower house of congress, the national service flag, familiar throughout the country, is given official recognition as such. Any organization is entitled to display the flag with a blue star for each of its members who is serving or has served in our military forces, a silver star for each member who has been wounded or captured and a gold star for each member who has been killed or died from the effects of wounds or disease. Relatives of soldiers may display the flag and wear the national service badge, similar in design to the flag, which is also given official recognition in the bill.

The bill goes further, as it should and makes unauthorized use of the flag or badge punishable by a fine or imprisonment.

Patriot Shield Quilt, c. 1917, 62 inches x 80 inches, cotton. This quilt was made by the mother of a World War I soldier while he was serving on the battlefront. Courtesy of Sandy Sutton.

Patriot Shield Quilt, c. 1917, 14 inches x 14 inches, cotton. This small quilt honors the service and role of the horse on the battlefront in World War I.

The Newark Advocate
Newark, Ohio
August 31, 1918, page 7

The W.R.C. will give a social on the court house lawn Labor Day, Sept. 2. The quilt in the Sperry & Harris window will be sold to the highest bidder, the proceeds to be used to buy a Liberty Bond. Public invited.

Oneonta Daily Star
Oneonta, New York
September 24, 1918, page 5

Handmade Service Flag

Mrs. Sarah Lyne made the Lincoln county (Kan.) service flag bearing its 300 stars, all of which are stitched on by hand instead of being pasted on, as is the usual method.

Kansas City Star
Kansas City, Missouri
November 23, 1918, page 1

Sell Quilt for Men's Dinner.

Now Battery D, 129th, Has $600 for a Christmas Deed.

Sisters and sweethearts of the soldier boys in Battery D, 129th Field Artillery, have sent them $600 for a Christmas dinner. In this battery are 190 young men from Kansas City. Each one of them will get the regulation Christmas gift box which the Government allows a relative to send but that is a small box, and a young man with a lively appetite might snap up in three bites all the Christmas cake and candy it would hold.

There was no government prohibition against sending money to the boys, so Miss Katherine Donnelly, Miss Loretta Gent, Miss Irene Gent, Miss Florence Conboy, Miss Anna Schweiger, Miss Florence Schweiger, Miss Gladys McCarthy, Miss Mary Tierney, Miss Theresa Tierney and Miss Norrine Quinlan together made a beautiful quilt And then called a dance of the old Cardinal Club at Drexell Hall. Fourteen members of the club are in Battery D in France, and so, there was

Today's Housewife, September, 1917, page 16.

deep interest when it was announced that the quilt would be auctioned at the dance. The quilt brought $600. The money has gone to France and there will be a "big chow" at Battery D's mess Christmas Day.

Trenton Evening Times
Trenton, New Jersey
December 10, 1918, page 5

Auxiliary Completes
Large Red Cross Quilt

FLEMINGTON, Dec. 10—The Ringoes Auxiliary of the American Red Cross has just completed a Red Cross quilt containing several hundred patches. Each of the patches contains the name of a person who donated 25 cents. More than $100 was raised in making the quilt which will be exhibited at the weekly meeting tomorrow. After that it will be exhibited at Larisons Corner, Reaville and Flemington.

Radiating Star Quilt, dated 1918, signed "Made for my son, T. Cox." 67 inches x 75 inches, cotton. This Radiating Star quilt features Eight-Point Stars along two opposing borders. The blue fabric in this quilt contains a very unstable dye. When it becomes slightly wet it bleeds into the surrounding areas. This may be due to the shortage of the high-quality German dyes favored by the textile industry prior to the war.

Jackson Citizen Patriot
Jackson, Michigan
March 14, 1919, page 14
Our Hero Boys
(The Poetry of It.)

> The cannon boom; make way, make room:
> Shrill high the fife; Today fills life
> With mother's joys;
> And beat the drum; for here they come,
> Our hero boys.
> The flag doth wave above the brave
> Who shrank not from a soldier's grave:
> The tried and true
> Who fought and bled beneath this red
> And white and blue.
> We see afar the wound, the scar,
> The empty sleeve, grim badge of war,
> The slow advance:
> The crippled limb where they got him
> Somewhere in France.
> Some medals rest upon the breast,
> We know the deeds that they attest—
> The laurel leaves;
> And silver stars and service bars
> Upon the sleeves.
> But now sad thought to us is brought—
> The company band so softly and
> So sweetly plays
> For those who will be absent still—
> Always, always!

Evansville Courier and Press
Evansville, Indiana
January 27, 1919, page 2
Boehne Camp Gets Quilt

> A quilt started for the soldiers by the Willing Workers of Parke Memorial church will go to Boehne camp, now that the Yanks no longer need warm bedding. The quilt was made by Miss Lottie Brote and twelve girls of her class.

Grand Forks Daily Herald
Grand Forks, North Dakota
February 27, 1919, page 3
Famous Army Quilt
Sold At Pembina

> Pembina, N.D., Feb. 26.—The famous Pembina county quilt, bearing the names of every boy who went to the army or navy from this county,

QUILT FOR RED CROSS KNITTED BY EIGHTEEN BOYS AND TWELVE GIRLS

Denver Post, Denver, Colorado, January 16, 1918, page 10. "A knitting corps composed of eighteen boys and twelve girls of the third grade at the Bromwell school have just completed a knitted quilt. It measures fifty-four inches square and contains eighty-one squares of different colors, and in the center are knitted the flags of the United States, Great Britain, France, Italy and Belgium.

"The children worked under the direction of Miss Adelaide de Weiss, their teacher, and the interest which the boys took is shown by the fact that more boys than girls participated in the making of the quilt. Besides making the quilt, the pupils of the Bromwell school have done much other work for the Red Cross, including fifty knitted garments and fifty handkerchiefs. The quilt also will be given to the Red Cross."

also the signature of President Wilson, was sold at auction at the picture theater here last Friday evening. The quilt was a most unique memento, beautifully wrought in silk. The proceeds of the sale went to the Red Cross.

Aberdeen American
Aberdeen, South Dakota
June 15, 1919, page 3
Jane's Crazy Quilt
By Eleanor Simmons

> Betty's Aunt Jane was not so very much older than was Betty herself, six turned twenty. But when Captain Burton, a young army officer en route home, stepped off at Glenn Centre to visit a friend at whose home, quite accidentally, he met Betty, and when she invited him over that evening for the sole purpose of writing his name on

World War I Fund Raiser Quilt. Denver, Colorado. Dated 1917-1918. 84 inches x 74 inches, machine pieced, hand embroidered, hand quilted, cotton. There are over 400 hundred signatures inscribed on this patriotic quilt from "The Great War."

The center of the quilt honors the men from the Denver area who fought in World War I. The soldiers' names are embroidered in blue. The Gold Stars represent men who were killed in action.

Aunt Jane's crazy quilt, the swift mental vision he had of Aunt Jane did not do justice to that most engaging young lady.

"It's like this," lisped Betty, "When our boys went to war they left vacancies that were hard to fill in this small town, so Aunt Jane—well, she just 'filled in' wherever she was needed most, and they kept her busy. The postmaster didn't have anyone to drive the mail when his son; Billy, went so Aunt Jane took the job until he found a man; and then she helped out at the corner grocery for a while, and the minute she was through there they sent word from the shoe store, "Would she please come over and help them out?" So while the rest of us kept house and sewed for the Red Cross she went from one man's job to another until she declared she would just have to do something feminine. So to relieve her feelings she started a crazy quilt. We call it a crazy quilt," went on Betty, "but, really, it is a beautiful thing—so soft and silky and cheery looking! All the neighbors brought in their odd silk and velvet pieces as soon as they found out she was making one. Maybe you think she might have used her spare time to better advantage but no one who knows how hard she worked to help win the war would begrudge her the only pleasure she allowed herself through it all. It will be sort of a war relic, too, when it is finished, for in the center of each square there will be a soldier's name in his own handwriting. Won't it be in-

The names of leaders in the W.C.T.U. are inscribed on this quilt. Some notable names on the quilt are Frances E. Willard, Carrie Nation, Lillian M. N. Stevens, Neal Dow, John B. Gough, W. J. Bryan, and Lady Sommerset.

cidentally learned a lesson so well herself that she had never been able to forget, although she gladly would have done so.

Many changes had occurred since then. The old home had been broken up, and she had come to this distant town to live with her sister; but through it all she had remembered.

Once again her heart pictured the tall young principal and listened to his earnest words of love. It was the proverbial lovers' quarrel that had come between them. She knew now that she had been to blame, but that realization came too late and no doubt another shared the heart and home which might have been hers but for her own foolish pride.

Betty's entrance into the room put an end to these reminiscent thoughts. "Oh, Aunt Jane," she began breathlessly; "I met an army captain this afternoon—the most splendid looking fellow—and he's coming over tonight to write his name on your quilt."

Tulsa World
Tulsa, Oklahoma
November 2, 1919, page 4
Patriotic Quilt
At Enid Exhibit
Names of all Garfield County Men
Who Saw War Service Placed
Upon Blanket.

ENID, Nov. 1—A patriotic quilt, containing the names of all Garfield county boys who saw service in the army during the recent war, is one of the special exhibits in the woman's work department at the Garfield county free fair and exposition in progress here. The idea is the property of Mrs. H. H. Miller 707 North Grant, Enid. The names are worked on blocks of red and white material. The blocks are four inches square. Names of the boys who fell in battle or died in service are embroidered in the center of the quilt.

teresting? When the boys come home they'll all have the honor of enrolling on Aunt Jane's quilt; but she'll feel proud to have a real captain's name on it the first thing, and you'll probably be instructed to write on the most conspicuous square of all. No we'll expect you this evening so don't disappoint us," concluded Betty, with her prettiest accent, and captain Burton smilingly assured her that he would be there at the appointed hour.

At home, Betty's mother was busily preparing supper, while her sister Jane sat by the window embroidering a beautiful silken square, "Seems good to have you home early, Jennie," said the elder woman. "Better put that work up now, though; this light's getting dim. Isn't that a piece of the dress you had that winter you taught school up in Maine?" "Yes," softly replied Jane as she folded her work and gazed dreamily out of the window, for that small piece of silk had awakened memories both pleasant and painful. It had taken her back to the little town where, six years before, she had taught the village school, and in-

Crazy Quilt, dated Dec. 1917, 58 inches x 66 inches, wool. The ship with the flag and "U.S.A."
indicates there may have been a sailor from the family in World War I.

Times–Picayune
New Orleans, Louisiana
November 21, 1919, page 19

**Miss Janvier's Quilt
Is A.E.F. History
Patchwork Comprises Insignia of Many Divisions of
Overseas Fighters.**

Army blankets are familiar sights, but army quilts are rare—so rare that New Orleans is said to boast the only one of its kind in existence. It is of the good, old-fashioned patchwork variety, and was quilted, padded and "pieced" by Miss Lois Janvier from 120 "patches" collected during her work abroad, representing almost every insignia of military life used in the A.E.F.

When our grandmothers did patchwork every fragment of sprigged dimity or cashmere in quaint design had a history of the garment it fashioned

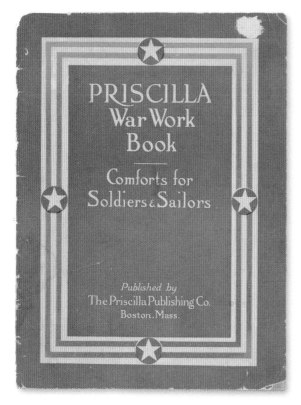

This booklet, priced at 25 cents, was published in 1917 by The Priscilla Publishing Company, Boston, Massachusetts. It featured instructions for providing needed articles of clothing for soldiers fighting in World War I. The instructions included: knitting articles of clothing such as mufflers, sweaters, helmets, socks and mittens; sewing hospital robes, pajamas, comfort kits and the highly recognized Red Cross quilt.

and the occasions on which it was worn. Stories that are woven in the world's history hang about the patchwork quilt that will hold a place of honor among the household goods of Miss Janvier when she marries Captain "Jack" Lester of Ohio in February.

Most of the patches were collected by soldiers who frequented her Y.M.C.A hut in Germany and had learned of their "colonel's" fad. One square, containing the insignia of the Railroad Artillery, represents the success of a search in which virtually the whole division joined. Few members of the

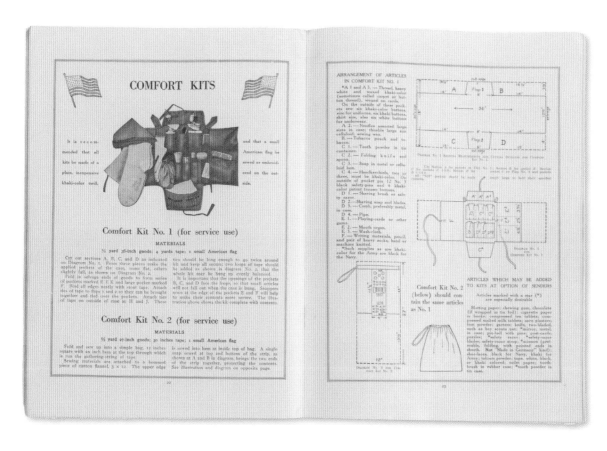

Trip Around the World Quilt, Navy Insignia Quilt, c. 1917, 84 inches x 80 inches, wool. This quilt was found in Maine.

R.A.R. had gone into Germany, but their insignia is one of the most fascinating of the A.E.F., a miniature railroad track circling the mythical mascot of the corps, the "Oozlefinch," a green bird with three wings and a wrist watch."

There are the two ferocious felines of the "Wildcat" Division, the littlest red ax of the "Railsplitting" Division, the Black Hawk of the Thirty-seventh; the little gold statue of Liberty of the Sev-

enty-seventh; the jolly yellow sun with the crown of the Advance Embarkation group; the loping grayhound of the courier service; the white cap of the army cooks; the triangles of the Tank Corps, and the streak of white lightening on a scarlet field that brought disgrace on a luckless second lieutenant of the Seventy-eighth Division who said in the hearing of his colonel who designed the insignia: "Well, guess it's all right if it's really meant to represent a white cat having spasms in a bottle of catsup."

The insignia are placed on black squares that alternate with vacant blue patches. In one corner Miss Janvier will place a miniature flag of D.H. Holmes Company, eighty silver and two gold stars to complete the record of her war experiences. Miss Janvier left her position as welfare director of the department store to do hut work in Germany as representative of the Louisiana Federation of Women's Clubs.

World War I Scripture Quilt, made by Emma Hembree, Cumberland City, Tennessee, started May 7, 1917, finished June 21, 1917, 67 inches x 93 inches, cotton. "Nearer, My God, to Thee" was written as a hymn by Sarah Flower Adams, an English poet and hymn writer in 1841, based on Jacob's Dream in Genesis 28:11. The hymn was often played at funerals of soldiers.

3. Under the Red Cross Flag

A Red Cross worker striking a dramatic pose in front of her Red Cross Fund Raising Quilt.

After the United States officially entered World War I on April 6, 1917 nearly 2.8 million American men were drafted into service. Throughout the next few months, President Wilson appealed to the American homefront to support and raise monies for the War Fund and the Roll Call campaigns through organizations like the Red Cross. These two national movements provided the major funding for the Red Cross. One of their most popular slogans was "We cannot serve in the trenches, but we can all serve at home." Americans enthusiastically responded by joining the ranks of supporters with a $1 membership. During the course of the War, over $250 million was raised for the relief effort abroad. The Roll Call solicited membership donations of $1 to successfully increase its members to 20 million people in two years' time.[22]

Idaho Statesman
Boise, Idaho
June 19, 1917, page 5
Women Selling Quilt
For Red Cross Fund
Disposing of Silk Gift Made by Old Woman; Design Has Symbolic Interest.

A number of local Red Cross workers are interesting themselves in the sale of the quilt which was made especially as a Red Cross donation by a charming old lady, now in her eighty-seventh year, who is of German descent, but who is so strongly pro-ally that she will not permit her name to be spelled in the German manner.

Shortly after the war was on and some time before the United States had entered it, this old lady, seeing a black and white Navajo rug with a Red Cross in the center, conceived the idea of making a quilt along the same design, since she was regarded as an expert quilter.

The quilt was finished last week and given to the Red Cross. It is an exquisite piece of work, made entirely of silk and has the Red Cross in the center, blue stars in the corners, representing "My Country," as the maker expressed it, and radiating from the Red Cross are yellow lines, which she designated as "the sunshine which my country has radiated through the Red Cross."

The story of the design, which was almost wholly original with the maker, is extremely poetic. The quilt is on exhibition at the Red Cross headquarters, and a group of workers is canvassing the women of the city—not a man will be permitted to buy a ticket—and they hope to dispose of it by the end of the week, to add the donation to the Red Cross county headquarters fund. Any woman interested who has a quarter to spare may see the quilt at headquarters.

The Iowa City Citizen
Iowa City, Iowa
June 26, 1917, page 1
Mrs. Franklin Kimball at the age of 92 made a quilt of the goose pattern and donated the same to the Red Cross society of Iowa City.

This quilt on account of the extreme age of the maker and the beauty of design, will attract widespread attention and will be on display at the Yetter store on Thursday of this week where it will be auctioned off to the highest bidder.

This Used to be the Bridge Club

—and many a jolly afternoon they had, too, with their aces, and hearts, and jacks, and no trumps.

Then the war came!

Brothers, and husbands, and sons, and sweethearts went away to become aces of the air, or jacks of the navy, or trumps of the American army.

The afternoon meetings continued—but the scenes changed to Red Cross workrooms—and serious, busy fingers of hundreds of thousands of patriotic American women have been making bandages and surgical dressings to alleviate the sufferings of their boys, and your boys, who responded so gallantly to the country's needs.

They are giving their time, their energy and their devotion to the cause of humanity, without stint or murmur.

And now comes your time to give your approval to the work your Red Cross has been doing.

Make this a Red Cross Christmas. Answer to the Red Cross Christmas Roll Call—December 16 to 23, and let the Christmas Eve Message to our men across the sea and our allies—and the thousands and thousands of stricken men, women and children of war-befouled areas—be that the American Nation stands solidly behind the Red Cross with universal membership, and that RED CROSS WORK WILL GO ON.

Join the Red Cross
All You Need is a Heart and a Dollar

Contributed Through Division of Advertising

United States Gov't Comm. on Public Information

This space contributed for the Winning of the War by
THE PUBLISHERS OF THE INDEPENDENT

Bids will be received each day and posted in the window and when there is no longer one who will raise the bid the quilt will be declared sold to the highest bidder.

The proceeds of the sale will be delivered to the Iowa City chapter of the Red Cross and thus a worthy cause will be advanced by the hand of the aged patriot.

The Iowa City Citizen
Iowa City, Iowa
June 27, 1917, page 2
"Goose Quilt"
Now On Display
Those who have not seen the "goose quilt" made by Mrs. Franklin Kimbal and on display in the window of the Yetter store, have missed something worth while. The

SUNBURST PATTERN QUILT NETS $206 FOR RED CROSS

Mrs. Will Thomas.   Mrs. E. L. Fodge.

Omaha World Herald, Omaha, Nebraska, May 26, 1918, page 8. "This quilt, one of the 'sunburst' pattern, proved highly lucrative for Red Cross purposes when a corps of Red Cross workers at the Brandeis store disposed of it for $206.25. This is the second quilt of the kind made by Mrs. Jane McManus for the Red Cross. It was awarded to 'No. 16.' The two women shown holding the quilt in the paragraph are: Mrs. Will Thomas, captain of the corps, and Mrs. E. L. Fudge, lieutenant."

Girls Make Red Cross Quilt

Fort Worth Star-Telegram, Fort Worth, Texas, August 13, 1918, page 2. "These are three patriotic little girls and their Red Cross quilt. The children are: Mabel Davis, 5, daughter of Mr. and Mrs. O.L. Davis, 1511 East Twentieth street; Alene Poe, 6, daughter of Mr. and Mrs. Tom Poe, 1601 East Twentieth street, and Latrell McKnney, 9, daughter of Mr. and Mrs. J.H. McKnney , 1516 East Twentieth street. By their own efforts the little girls made the quilt, which they have donated to the Red Cross. Their smiles show their pride in the accomplishment."

Auburn Women Piece Quilt For the Red Cross

Mrs. Ella Carper.   Mrs. Emma M. Mitchell.

The Fort Wayne News & Sentinel, Fort Wayne, Indiana, May 25, 1918, page 9. "Anxious to 'do their bit' toward making the world safe for democracy, Mrs. Ella Carper and Mrs. Emma A. Mitchell, of Auburn, pieced a quilt which they sold and turned the proceeds over to the Red Cross.

"Thirty-one dollars and nine cents were derived from the sale of the quilts, which sum was given to the Auburn Red Cross society. The women are quite proud of their achievement, but feel that this is but a mite as compared to what our boys are doing over there.

"Both of the ladies have relatives in the service. Mrs. Mitchell has two sons in the 127th U.S. Field Artillery, Battery B, and Mrs. Carper has two grandsons in the same company. The boys are stationed at camp Bailey."

Red Cross Quilt, 1918, made by the Pythian Sisters, Phoenix, Arizona, to raise money for the Red Cross. 84 inches x 95 inches, cotton. This quilt was made to follow the pattern published by *The Modern Priscilla Magazine*, December, 1917. Collection of the Arizona Historical Society, Central Arizona Division Museum.

figures are in white on a field of blue the whole being bordered with white and beautifully quilted. This piece of work will be sold to the highest bidder and the entire proceeds to the Red Cross.

Morning Olympian
Olympia, Washington
August 23, 1917, page 3

Red Crosses on a white background bordered in the navy blue of the flag is the pattern of the "Red Cross Quilt" now being displayed by the Olympia Red Cross society. It was made and donated to the local chapter by Mrs. John Gunstone, of South Union. Although the Red Cross committee has not definitely decided what it will do

it is possible that a "Red Cross Quilt Raffle," will be held soon.

Oregonian
Portland, Oregon
October 13, 1917, page 12
What You Can Make
At Home
By Mrs. Portland.

Blocks for a Red Cross pattern quilt are very easily made. From any kind of red goods, silk, cotton or woolen, cut an oblong piece of cloth six inches long and two inches wide. Also from the same red goods cut two squares two by two inches. From similar white or light-colored goods cut four squares two by two inches.

Sew each of the two red squares to two light-colored squares, placing the

> *This Liberty Quilt was started by Mrs. Martha F. Brunner of Hartford, Conn., in 1918, to raise money for the Red Cross, as a patriotic service in honor of our brave men and women in our country's service.*
>
> *It was planned and made by Mrs. Alice M. Jones and Mrs. M. C. Brott of the Ladies Aid Society of the Windsor Ave. Congregational Church of Hartford, Conn. The names were inscribed by Miss Waters.*
>
> *The amount raised for the Red Cross by means of this quilt was*
> *$1150.*

Close-up of the center bottom square of the Connecticut Red Cross quilt explains the making of the quilt and the amount of monies raised for the Red Cross. The label identifies it as "The Liberty Quilt."

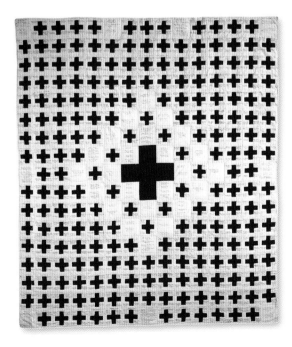

Red Cross Quilt, c. 1918, made by The Ladies' Aid Society of the Windsor Avenue Congregational Church, Hartford, Connecticut. 83 inches x 94 inches, cotton. Courtesy of The Connecticut Historical Society, Hartford, Connecticut. Acc #A.1622

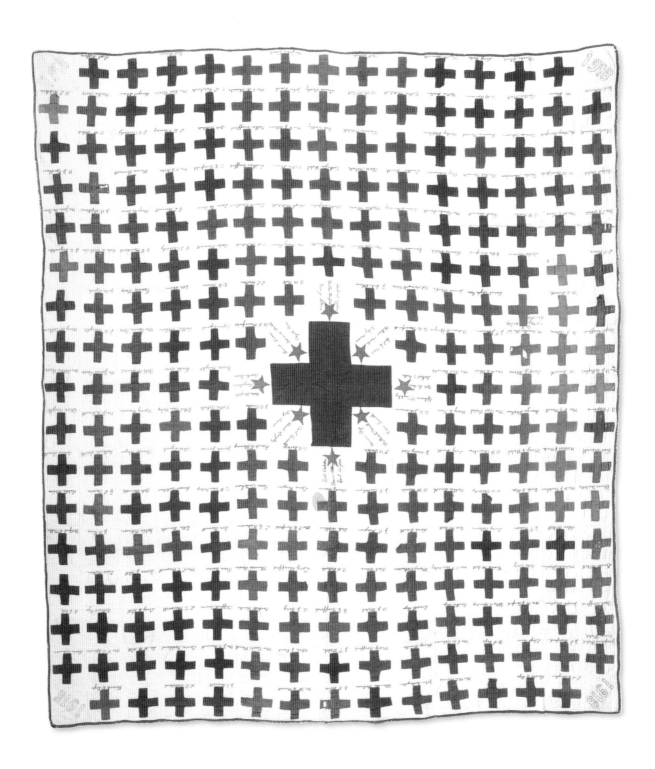

Central Ohio Red Cross Quilt, dated 1918, 86 inches x 78 inches, cotton.
The names around the Blue Stars represent World War I soldiers.

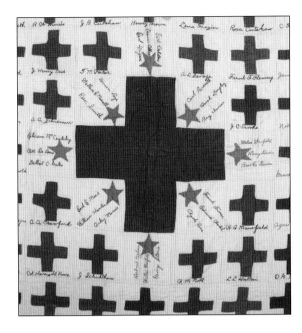

red square between the two light-colored squares. You will now have three strips, one of plain red six inches long and two composed of red and light-colored blocks sewed together. Of course there must always be allowance made for seams by cutting any piece just a little larger according to the width of seam you are accustomed to make in such work. Sew the three strips together, putting the plain red strip in the middle. This will give you a square block with white or light-colored squares in each of the four corners and with a red cross in the center at right angles to the edges of the block.

The blocks may be set together to form a quilt top by placing white or light-colored six-inch squares between them and sewing the strips thus formed together vertically or horizontally; or diagonal strips may be made by-which method red crosses would extend diagonally over the quilt top. Or the blocks may be set together with narrow strips instead of squares, making them two or four inches wide.

It is seldom advisable to mix widely different kinds of goods in a quilt, not only because the wearing qualities are so different but also because differ-

ent kinds of cloth require such diverse methods of cleaning. Heavy woolens should be used together, but not in the same blocks with lightweight woolens. Silks, linens and cottons are better separate, though linens and cottons may be used together. Hand sewing in piecing quilts is usually more satisfactory than machine stitching, but if the machine stitching is used, the ends of the thread should be securely tied whenever cut or broken. A woolen quilt may have a cotton lining because a woolen lining will often make it too heavy to handle easily, and to give additional stoutness, silk and light cotton quilt tops may be lined with heavier cotton goods. On account of its excellent wearing qualities, unbleached muslin makes a good quilt lining.

Aberdeen Daily News
Aberdeen, South Dakota
October 27, 1917, page 5
Ipswich Woman Gives
Quilt To Red Cross

Word has come from Ipswich that Mrs. Victor Strum of that city has donated a beautiful quilt of the old fashioned log cabin design to the Red Cross. It is said that the ladies expect to realize almost as much money out of this quilt to purchase materials for the Edmunds county chapter of the Red Cross as the Parmley pony brought the state organization at the state fair.

Iowa City Citizen
Iowa City, Iowa
December 1, 1917, page 8
All Honor Due
Aged Workers
Of Red Cross
Quilt Made by Aged Iowa
City Woman Nets $212 for
Red Cross

Kathleen Majoribanks, a literary woman of Chicago and former Iowa City woman writes the *Citizen* of the great work for the American Red Cross being done by one of Iowa City's most honored women, Mrs. Lydia Kimball.

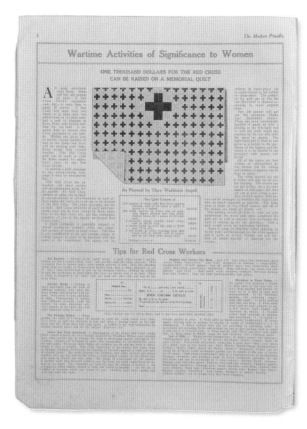

"Wartime Activities of Significance to Women." *The Modern Priscilla Magazine,* December, 1917, page 2. The publication of this quilt pattern, combined with the call from President Woodrow Wilson to raise monies for the Red Cross, precipitated an intense national effort making quilts for the Red Cross. Hundreds of communities of quiltmakers nationwide followed the Modern Priscilla design or incorporated the Red Cross in their own design. These quilts raised thousands of dollars for the Red Cross to benefit our soldiers during World War I.

Patriotic Woman Helps Cause.

Mrs. Kimball is now ninety-three years of age and is still active in the work of the country. During the past few months she has kept her needle busy and many knitted garments as well as quilts and the like have been made and the proceeds turned in to the Red Cross, or the garment given to the relief of the soldiers. During the summer, a beautiful "goose" quilt, the work of her hands, was placed on sale at Yetters' store and the proceeds turned into the Red Cross.

Not the First Time

More than a half a century ago Mrs. Kimball was active in the work of the Red Cross, or "Ladies' Aid" as it was then called, and to-

gether, with many other women of the country including Mrs. Samuel Kirkwood, still living in this city and widow of Iowa's civil war governor, did much for the relief of the soldiers at the front. The following letter from Miss Majoribanks is self explanatory:

The Letter

"2306 N Clark St.
"November 24th, 1917
"Editor, Iowa City Citizen,
"Iowa City, Iowa

"Dear Sir

"When I think of the wonderful work that women all over the country are doing for the Red Cross I feel like climbing to the top of the highest mountain and crying, "Well done." And when I think of the work done by the oldest of our women whose lives are mostly spent in memories, I feel like adding a cheer to cry.

"The impulse was very strong within me when, three months ago, I received a beautiful hand made Blue Bird quilt from Mrs. Lydia Kimball of Iowa City—your townswoman and my dear friend—with the simple message that she wanted to do something for the Red Cross and this was all she 'could do.'

"'All she could do' meant, in this instance, $212 toward real help and comfort to the men who are fighting our battle with a willingness to lay down their lives if necessary —four thousand miles from home! The quilt came to me just as I was leaving for the west and I took it with me until I could decide which unit of the Red Cross to send it to. Arriving in Wyoming I found that the Dayton Auxiliary was the nearest, and that this was desperately in need of funds to provide the necessary materials for the work the members were so willing to do— dressings, towels, pajamas, shirts etc, etc Mrs. Jack Milward of The Grange, Dayton secretary of the branch, took the quilt over, and

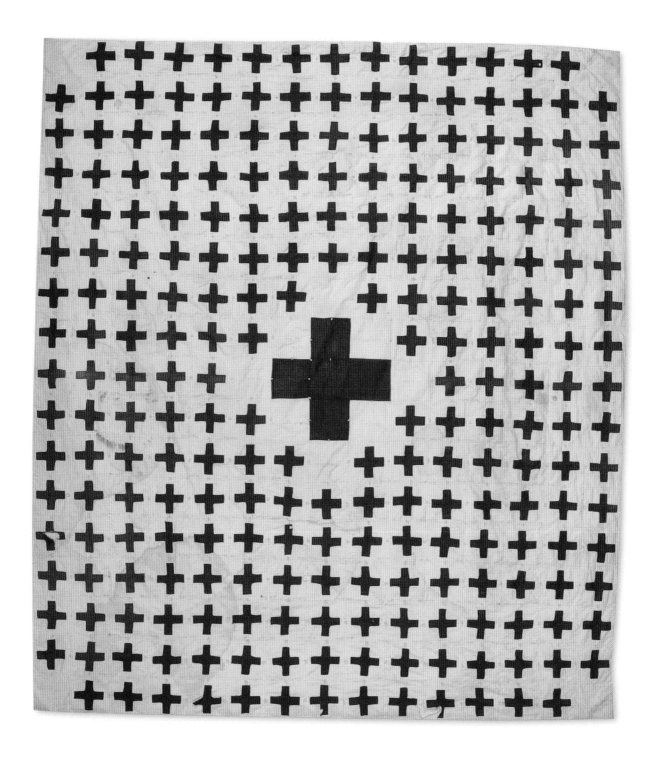

Red Cross Quilt, c. 1918, Rutland, Vermont, 96 inches x 87 inches, cotton. The Red Cross pattern was designed by Clara Washburn Angell of *The Modern Priscilla* magazine. It was published in the December 1917 issue in response to a call for increased fund raising for the Red Cross and the War effort.

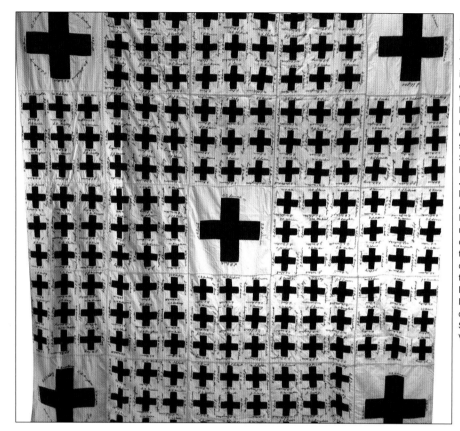

Red Cross Quilt, made by Senannie Beaty (1892–1987), Greene County, Virginia, 82 inches x 82 inches, cotton. The embroidery (and most likely the piecing) was the work of Miss Senannie Beaty, a renowned volunteer in her community. The center square carries Miss Senannie's name (S. R. Beaty) as well as those of John Owen Beaty, her brother, and her aunts, Adeline Cornelia Simms and Elizabeth Davis Simms. The names of notable area citizens were inscribed on the quilt. Many people donated money for more than one square. C. B. Dulaney's name appears at least twelve times. Courtesy of Greene County Historical Society, Stanardsville, Virginia.

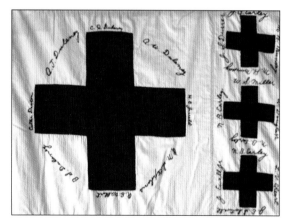

Miss Senannie Beaty, Greenville County, Virginia.

Red Cross Quilt, Burbank, Ohio, dated 1918, 72 inches x 70 inches, cotton. This is yet another variation of the Red Cross quilt of the Modern Priscilla version published in December, 1917.

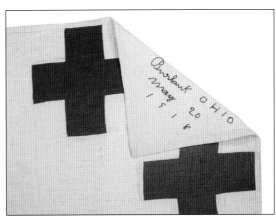

Inscription on the back of the quilt.

The Red Cross Magazine cover, March 1918.

The Ladies' Home Journal Magazine, September, 1917, page 5. This article shows the variety of dress required for volunteer Red Cross workers.

through her efforts the large sum was realized.

"She sold raffle tickets at twenty-five cents apiece, until a hundred dollars were in sight. Then, on an appointed day she invited the whole countryside to tea on her lawn where she went to endless trouble to provide decorations, and every attraction and comfort imaginable for those who wanted to come. Tea, cakes, lemonade, and ices were on sale—the sales amounting to $78.00 all of which went to the Red Cross fund. To 'do her bit' a neighbor, Mrs. Graham, lent her motor car and personally ran it from Dayton to the Milward house, charging a nickel a trip for those who could not walk the distance thereby adding ten dollars to the fund. When the crowd of 169 were assembled on the lawn, the tickets were turned over in a beautiful old churn, decorated with flags and bunting. Miss Adelaide Coleman of Springfield was declared the winner, and immediately she hand-

ed the quilt over to Mr. Harry Mc-Cormick of Omaha who, in the most professional way, auctioned it off to Mr. Thomas Hughes, the IXL ranch, Dayton, Wyoming, for twenty-four dollars. More money for the fund.

"And there you have the story of $212 for the American Red Cross. All honor to Mrs. Kimball, Miss Milward, Miss Coleman, and Mr. McCormick.

I cannot help feeling that this story will hold interest for you an American, and I hope, a member of the Red Cross, so I am sending it without apology for taking up the time of a busy man."

"Yours very truly,
KATHLEEN MAJORIBANKS"

This postcard shows a hometown parade of Red Cross workers during World War I.

Iowa Recorder
Greene, Iowa
January 1, 1918, page 13

At the second Red Cross sale $160.30 was netted making the amount $2292. 22. The Red Cross quilt given by the Even Dozen club has over 1000 names written in indelible ink.

Aberdeen Daily News
Aberdeen, South Dakota
January 3, 1918, page 4

Barnard Will Stage Field Day For R.c.

Saturday, January 12, is going to be a red letter day for Red Crossdom in the little city of Barnard. The day will be devoted to activities for the Red Cross and is to be known as field day. Farmers will bring in their produce for an auction sale and according to authentic reports, the town and vicinity are running over with enthuseiasm over the prospective event.

A notable feature of the day will be the raffling of a beautiful silk quilt fashioned by the clever fingers of

Mrs. Donald Strachan, Sr., who is 70 years old, the mother of eleven children and has lived there since 1884. This estimable woman has already sold numbers on the quilt equivalent to $102.50.

Olympia Daily Recorder
Olympia, Washington
January 11, 1918, page 2

Who Will Win the Red Cross Quilt?

A handsome Red Cross quilt, the work of Mrs. John Gunstone, will be given to the luckiest person who attends the Red Cross benefit dance tomorrow night at the Tumwater club house.

A chance on the quilt will be given to each person purchasing a ticket and during the course of the evening the lucky number will be drawn.

The quilt is fashioned from the national colors. It is edged with blue and has 25 red

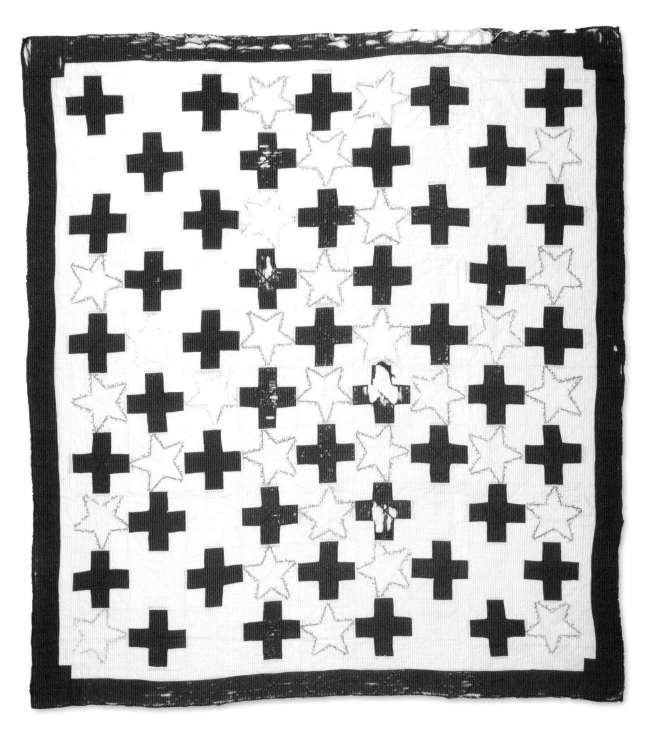

Red Cross and Star Quilt, c. 1918, 72 inches x 81 inches, hand appliquéd, hand embroidered, cotton. Courtesy of Cynthia Adams.

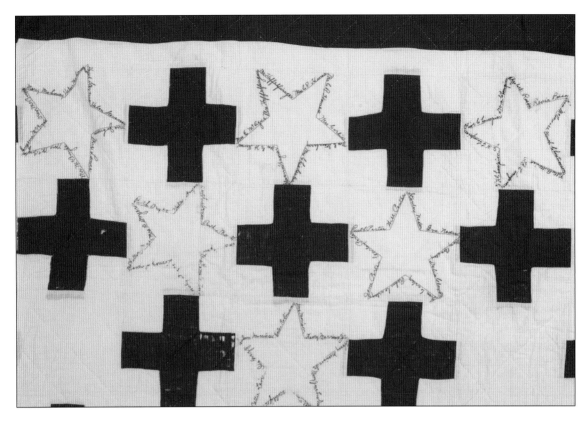

1918 Red Cross church scene from Commerce, Georgia.

1918 Red Cross workroom at Schenley High School, Pittsburgh, Pennsylvania.
"Finding a Way," *The Red Cross Magazine,* October, 1918, page 61.

crosses worked on a background of white. Everyone present will have a chance, an equal chance with every other person. Raymond's seven piece orchestra will furnish the music for the dance.

Idaho Statesman
Boise, Idaho
March 2, 1918, page 7
Red Cross Quilt Will
Net the Chapter $1009
Mrs. A.B. Golden and Mrs. Calvin Crane, two expert needlewomen, are at work upon a Red Cross quilt, from which they expect to realize $1009.

The quilt will be made of red and white material, red crosses upon a white ground on one side and plain white blocks on the reverse side. There are 226 blocks on each side, and the plan is to embroider four names on each block. For the smaller blocks the names will come to 25 cents each, and the larger ones vary from $5 to $50 per block.

If all the blocks are taken, the result will be $1009; which will be turned over to the Red Cross, together with the quilt, which can then be disposed of as the chapter sees fit.

The materials for the quilt have been donated by the Falk Mercantile company and the receipt blanks for names by the Sums-York company.

Although there will be an immense amount of work to be done, the needle workers expect to have the quilt finished in time for the May Red Cross drive.

Seattle Daily Times
Seattle, Washington
April 28, 1918, page 7
Quilt Brings $700
To Red Cross Chest
WALLA WALLA, Saturday, April 27. —At an auction held this week at the city, a Red Cross quilt was gold for $700. The event occurred at the Clifford Riggs ranch, and farmers from all over that section attended.

The quilt is a beautiful piece of

Trip Around The World, c. 1915, 76 inches x 76 inches, cotton.

workmanship, being made of scarlet Red Cross emblems upon a pure white ground. After the quilt had been sold time and again and when $700 had been taken in the sale was stopped, and the quilt was donated by the last purchaser to the Red Cross Auxiliary at Touchet, a nearby town. The quilt will again be sold at auction at the Touchet Liberty Loan program next week.

Wyoming State Tribune
Cheyenne, Wyoming
May 3, 1918, page 6

The Junior Red Cross of the Cheyenne high school is doing effective work under the management of Miss Alice Williamson and Miss Valeria Bonnell, two popular members of the faculty. At present the girls of the junior organization are fashioning a quilt for hospital use in France. It may be of interest to the readers of Red Cross. The dimensions are 6 x 4 feet, and composed of twenty-four blocks of alternate white and rose colored cotton cloth, each 12 x 12 inches. On the white blocks are placed in appliqué, in rose color, the legend "C. H.S." and a red cross, these legends occupying alternate white blocks. The appliqué is hemmed in small stitches and the effort is indescribably beautiful.

Jackson Citizen Patriot
Jackson, Michigan
May 6, 1918, page 8

Fifty-three ladies attended the North Leoni Red Cross meeting in the grange hall this week. Eleven pajamas suits and several housewives were finished: two pair of socks, one sweater and three pair of wristlets were turned in and three quilts were finished. Dinner was served to twenty-nine at noon. This branch is in a very thriving condition, a great deal of interest being shown in the work even at this busy time of year.

Oregonian
Portland, Oregon
May 19, 1918, page 52

Grandma's Quilt Brings $5000.

PENDLETON, Or., May 18.—(Special.)—Word has been received here that the red, white and blue satin quilt made by Grandma Hoon, of Umapine, 13 years ago for the St. Louis World's Fair, has been sold by the Red Cross in Washington, D.C., for $5000. It won an award at the fair and again at the Seattle Exposition. Its buyers plan to return it to the Red Cross to be sold again. It probably will be sent to all states in this country to be auctioned.

Evening Star
Washington D.C.
May 19, 1918, page 30
and
Times-Picayune
New Orleans, Louisiana
May 20, 1918, page 5

Autograph Quilt for Red Cross.

A Red Cross autograph quilt containing the signatures of President Wilson, Vice President Marshall, members of the cabinet, senators, representatives, governors of many states, and other Americans will be sold at auction for the ambulance fund being raised by the Junior Red Cross of Alexandria, Va., the Red Cross Bulletin announces. The autographs are inscribed with waterproof inks on the white blocks of the quilt, which is being made by Mrs. John Edward Nevin, wife of a Washington newspaper correspondent.

The Newark Advocate
Newark, Ohio
June 29, 1918, page 6

Granville

All those interested in the disposal of the patriotic quilt made by the Pioneer Relief club from pieces of garments worn by the children composing the "Living Flag" at the Centennial cele-

Walla Walla Union Bulletin, Walla, Walla, Washington, July 4, 1976, page 5. "Forest R. Leedy of Wenatchee displays a patriotic quilt he won in a 1918 Red Cross raffle. It is sewn from 146 quilt blocks, each with a red cross on a white background."

bration, are invited to the King's Daughters rooms this evening at 7 o'clock. You will find the exercises interesting. The money realized is for war relief.

Times-Picayune
New Orleans, Louisiana
June 2, 1918, page 11B
Girls Make Quilt
From Flag Scraps

An old-fashioned patch-work quilt, made from remnants of material used in making Red Cross flags, is displayed as a practical demonstration of thrift by students of Esplanade High School. The squares were made by students, put together and quilted by Miss B.R. Van Horn of the faculty and presented to the New Orleans chapter of the Red Cross.

The Newark Advocate
Newark, Ohio
June 29, 1918, page 6
Granville

A delightful little program was given Friday evening in The King's Daughters' rooms by the members of the Pioneer Relief club, in connection with the disposal of the patriotic quilt for war relief funds. Mrs. McLaughlin secured the quilt with much applause. The amount raised $17.50, will be divided between the local Red Cross and the King's Daughters, with five dollars retained by the Pioneers.

Evansville Courier and Press
Evansville, Indiana
July 14, 1918, page 7
Grayville Society

A Red Cross quilt containing 1,057 names has been completed here. The quilt contains a large Red Cross in the center, with the names of 100 soldier boys from this city grouped around it. The names of 957 citizens of this vicinity form the border of the quilt. The proceeds, together with the sum charged each person for the placing of their name on the quilt, will be given to the Red Cross.

Daily Illinois State Register
Springfield, Illinois
August 15, 1918, page 9
Red Cross Is
Shown At Work
Fine Display That Appeals
Patriotism To Be Seen
At State Fair.

The American Red Cross, "The Greatest Mother in the World" who has enthroned herself in the hearts of 100,000,000 people is shown at work amid beautiful surroundings in the balcony of the Exposition building in the State Fair grounds. Beautiful, not because of costly furnishings but because of the spotless purity of the entire booth - all done in snow white clad women in charge. The severity of the white being relieved merely by the red cross the in-

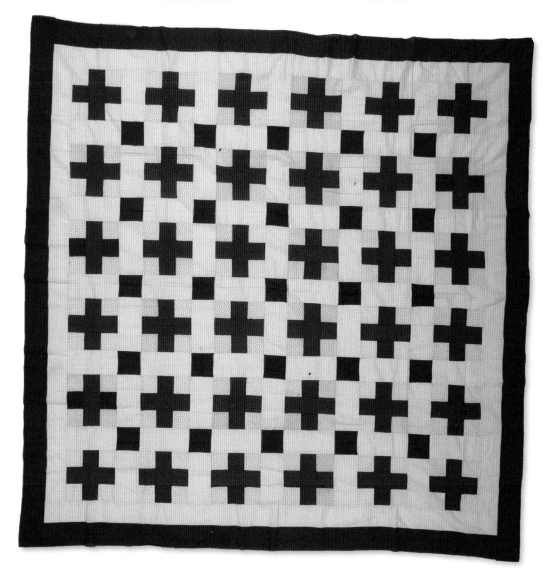

Red Cross Quilt Top, c. 1918, 78 inches x 78 inches, cotton. Red Cross quilts
were popular from about late 1917 to 1919 during the World War I years, making them easy to date.

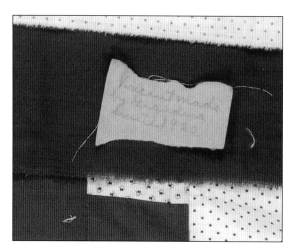

Label sewn to the back of the quilt top.

signia of this great organization of mercy. The appeal of that red cross on its field of white is a strong one, speaking as it does of the service which its wearer renders to the lads over there.

Samples of all branches of Red Cross work are on display, representing the labor of the units from all parts of the state. The exhibit includes surgical dressings, refugee garments, infant layettes, hospital garments and numerous others all of which will be sent to Central Division at the close of the fair for distribution. One feature of particular interest is a Red Cross quilt from the Red Cross unit of Ramsey, Ill., where it was sold at auction for $250. The quilt is composed of blocks bearing about 500 signatures of prominent Illinois persons, among them Governor and Mrs. Lowden, and Adjutant General Dickson.

A Red Cross worker is striking a patriotic pose on this silk pillow cover from World War I.

This magnificent, embroidered Red Cross Sampler Quilt depicts World War I symbols, scenes and images popularly found in magazines and newspapers in 1917 to 1919. It is a remarkable wartime textile documenting the essence of the homefront contribution to the war effort. Courtesy of Conference Archives Library & Museum, Lovely Lane United Methodist Church, Baltimore, Maryland.

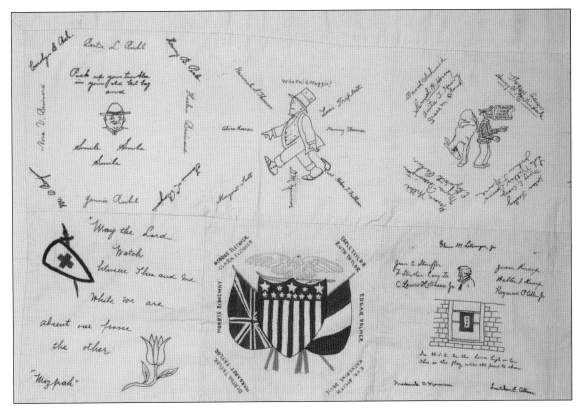

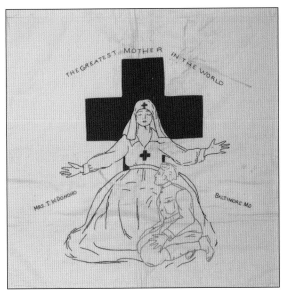

Images in World War I era magazines such as *National Geographic* inspired the center motif of the Lovely Lane Church quilt.

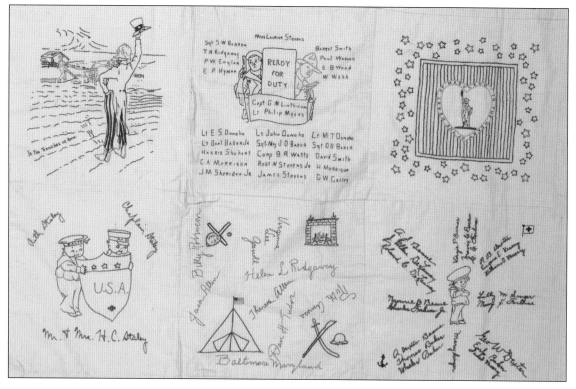

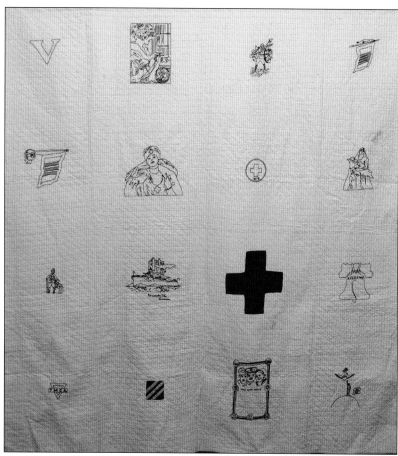

World War I Sampler Quilt, c. 1919, 67 inches x 69 inches, cotton. One of the Redwork blocks on this quilt was inscribed with "Remember the *Tuscania*." The *Tuscania* was a British troopship sunk February 15, 1918. Other blocks depict soldiers, nurses, flags, a Red Cross, the Liberty Bell and the Statue of Liberty. Courtesy of the New England Quilt Museum (#2013.36).

Salt Lake Telegram
Salt Lake City, Utah
August 30, 1918, page 9
Bamberger's Name
Asked For Square
On Red Cross Quilt

Governor Simon Bamberger has been asked for his signature on one of the squares of a Red Cross quilt, being made by the pupils of the seventh and eighth grades of the Santa Monica school, Los Angeles, Cal., which will be placed on exhibition this fall at the Liberty fair in Los Angeles. A letter to Governor Bamberger from Miss Eva A. Jones recites that signatures for squares have been obtained from President and Mrs. Wilson, Herbert C. Hoover, Gener- Al Leonard Wood, Maude Adams, Mary Pickford and the governors of several states. On the square sent to Governor Bamberger are the signatures of Governors Arthur Capper of Kansas, Charles Henderson of Alabama, W.P. Hobby of Texas and Charles H. Brough of Arkansas.

Oneonta Daily Star
Oneonta, New York
September 24, 1918, page 6

Mrs. Lyne has also pieced a "Red Cross" quilt, which the Methodist Ladies' society has quilted, and the quilt is soon to be sold at auction for the Red Cross.

Tampa Tribune
Tampa, Florida
September 26, 1918, page 8

To Piece Quilt for Belgians—The Red Cross Auxiliary of the Palm Avenue Baptist church will meet Thursday morning with Mrs. Kate Crilly, corner of Florabraska avenue and Taliaferro street, and all the ladies are asked to bring scraps of outing flannel to piece together for a quilt for the Belgium relief work. All those having old clothes to give for this purpose are also requested to bring it at this time, so that it may be sent all together to headquarters.

Fort Worth Star-Telegram
Fort Worth, Texas
October 9, 1918, page 13
Red Cross Quilt
Made Of Soldiers'
Neckties Net $240

A Red Cross quilt made of silk neckties, belonging to soldiers now on the battlefield was the contribution of the Euless-Tarrant Red Cross Auxiliary. The quilt was sold and netted $240 for the Red Cross. Mrs. H.G. Walker is chairman of the Auxiliary.

World War I Fund Raising Quilt, c. 1918, East Hanover, Dauphin County, Pennsylvania, 72 inches x 72 inches, cotton. The hundreds of names were penned on this quilt to raise monies for the Red Cross. It is clear from the amount recorded in the center of each block just how much money was raised for the war effort. Courtesy of Laura Fisher.

World War I, Red Cross Quilt. East St. Louis, Illinois. Dated 1919, 74.5 inches x 70.5 inches, machine pieced, hand embroidered, hand quilted, cotton. This quilt was made for fund raising during World War I. The names embroidered on the quilt helped to raise money for the Red Cross. The names of soldiers are featured with Red Stars and Gold Stars. The center inscription suggests the quilt was made to welcome home the 124th Field Artillery at the war's end.

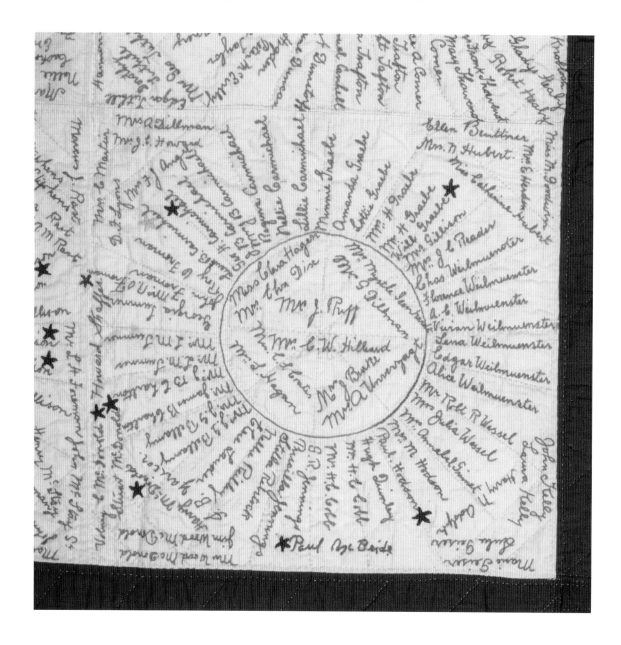

The Humeston New Era
Humeston, Iowa
October 23, 1918, page 6
Quilt Sells for $15

 Corydon Times-Republican: A Red Cross quilt made by a group of northwest Jefferson and southwest Clay townships, was presented to the Wayne County, Chapter of the Red Cross and sold at public auction Saturday evening. J.D. Sharp, one of our well known farmers and race horsemen, who has four boys in the army, bought the quilt paying $15 for the same.

Flint Journal
Flint, Michigan
December 4, 1918, page 8

 The Red Cross fair will be held at the hall on Dec. 11. It is expected the "name" Red Cross quilt will then be auctioned off. It was first planned to send the quilt to Camp Custer.

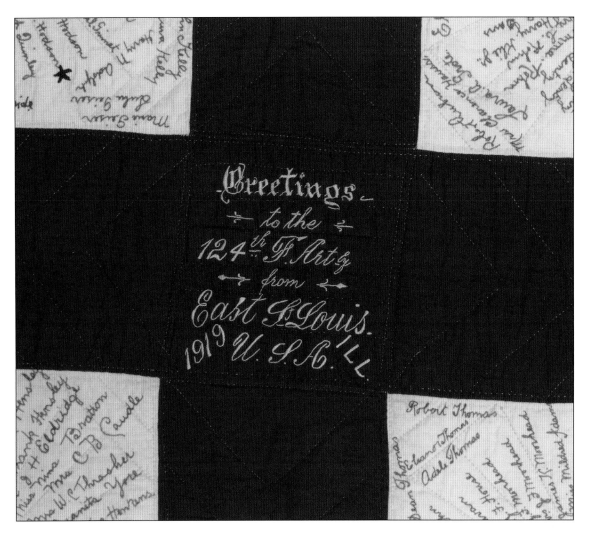

Duluth News–Tribune
Duluth, Minnesota
December 22, 1918, page 3
Emerson Mothers' Club

The Mothers' club of the Emerson school held their regular meeting at the school Wednesday afternoon. Victory songs were sung by the pupils of the seventh grade, followed by an informal farewell talk by the principal, Miss Mabel Rossman, who is leaving very soon to enter the service of the government. A feature of the afternoon was the raffling of a Red Cross quilt. This quilt, which is a white one with red stars was pieced by the members at their Red Cross circle meetings. The sum of $43 was realized, which will be used in relief work in the Emerson school district.

Twin Falls News
Twin Falls, Idaho
January 14, 1919, page 5
Quilt Sale For Benefit
(Special to The News)

KIMBERLY—The Red Cross quilt made by the young women of the Methodist church and quilted by the "service star" mothers of men in the army and navy, is to be sold in accordance with a plan which has been worked out for the benefit of the local Red Cross hospital.

Woodlands Daily Democrat
Woodland, California
February 21, 1919, page 1
Handsome Quilt Given Red Cross by Mrs. John Ruppert

Mrs. John Rupport has donated a quilt to the Red Cross shop. It is a

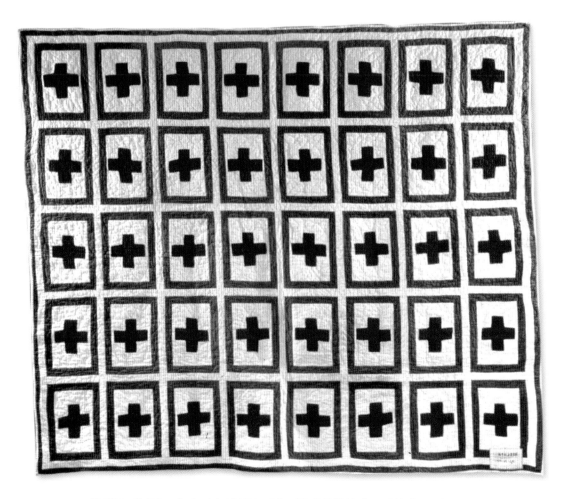

Red Cross Quilt, Inscribed on label "M.E. Lord, Age 82, 1919," 64 inches x 74 inches, cotton.
There are two concentric hearts quilted in the center of each cross. Courtesy of New England Quilt Museum (#1991.33).

very durable and handsome article. Batting for the quilt was donated by Griggs & Bush, lining by Fred Wirth and thread by the Racket Store.

Record Herald
Waynesboro, Pennsylvania
March 8, 1919, page 1

Credit Junior Red Cross and Women of Church of Brethren For Fine Quilt In Besore Window

Job was a patient man. But he was a man. For patient women come to Waynesboro. For an example of patience try and count the stitches in the quilt in the show window of the Besore Dry Goods company. In the center of the quilt is a large red cross with a white background. Radiating from the center are 52 patches, each one eight inches square. In each patch are 20 names, each letter in each name embroidered in red —all hand work. Around the entire quilt is a blue border four inches wide. Each name represents 10 cents—the amount given by the man or woman whose name appears in red thread. The Junior Red Cross raised the money—sold the names at 10 cents each.

The Woman's Aid Society of the Church of the Brethren did the quilting.

Many thousands of stitches—perhaps more than a hundred thousand—are in the quilt. To do that work required patience.

There were three of these quilts. The patches for the others were sent to the Philadelphia chapter of the Red Cross, where they will be sewed in an old ladies' home.

Red Cross Quilt, c. 1918, Unknown quiltmaker. Tennessee. 78 inches x 85 inches, cotton. There are six to eight names inscribed on each of the blocks and multiple names on the border. Unfortunately none of the names include a date or place name. Courtesy of New England Quilt Museum #2012.24.

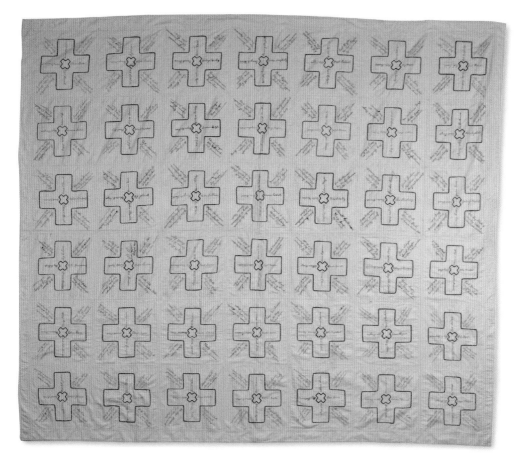

Red Cross Quilt, 1916, made by the women of Martell, Nebraska. 672 residents of Martell, Nebraska, paid 50 cents to have their names signed on the quilt. A total of $411 was raised with the making and auction of this quilt. 72 inches x 84.5 inches. Courtesy of The Nebraska State Historical Society, Lincoln, Nebraska (11694-1).

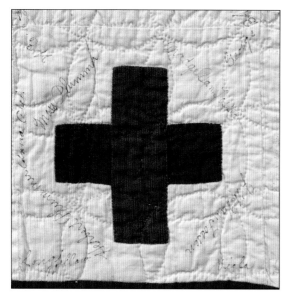

Aberdeen Daily News
Aberdeen, South Dakota
April 3, 1919, page 4
Red Cross Receives Interesting Quilt

The Brown county chapter of the Red Cross yesterday was presented with a quilt made by the women of the Bethlehem Lutheran Ladies' Aid society.

The quilt, which is made in blocks, is of white and embroidered in red is several hundred names of the women of the society and their friends. Each woman gave toward the Red Cross a sum of 10 cents and her name was then embroidered on the quilt. In all $86.91 was collected and this also given to the Red Cross yesterday. It is expected that the quilt will be placed on exhibition soon.

AFTERWARD
POPPY QUILTS:
THE FIELDS OF FLANDERS

We Shall Keep the Faith
Moina Michael, 1918

>Oh! You who sleep in Flanders Fields,
>Sleep sweet—to rise anew!
>We caught the torch you threw
>And holding high, we keep the Faith
>With All who died.
>We cherish, too, the Poppy red
>That grows on fields where valor led,
>It seems to signal to the skies
>That blood of heroes never dies,
>But lends a luster to the red
>Of the flower that blooms above the dead
>In Flanders Fields.
>And now the Torch and Poppy Red
>We wear in honor of our dead.
>Fear not that ye have died for naught;
>We'll teach the lesson that ye wrought
>In Flanders Fields.

American Moina Michael, author of the poem "We Shall Keep the Faith," is honored as the Founder of the Memorial Day Poppy.[23] In the early 1920s, American Legions began to observe Poppy Day. The red flowers were made of paper, often by soldiers of the war disabled by combat. Veterans in hospitals, and often blinded by chemical warfare, made near perfect poppies. They were paid 1 cent for each flower made. The poppy flower quickly won the hearts of all survivors of the war worldwide.

The true reason for the adoption of the poppy as the memorial flower for World War I is little known. In the spring of 1919 throughout France and the Low Country, amidst complete devastation, the poppies bloomed in abundance on the battlefields where so many met their deaths.[24]

The VFW (Veterans of Foreign Wars) adopted the poppy as its official flower in 1922. In 1924, a poppy factory was built in Pittsburgh, providing another source for the commemorative

A post–World War I, Flanders Field parade float honoring the soldiers of World War I buried in the many small cemeteries scattered throughout France and Belgium. Poppies and white crosses decorate the platform.

flower.[25] Even today, wearing the poppy signifies honor for those who lost their lives in the "Great War."

In the 1920s, Poppy quilts became a popular choice of botanical quilts. Red, white and green and red, white and blue were the preferred color combinations. The new emerging quilt designers and pattern companies responded with appliquéd poppies designed in bouquets, wreaths, swags and baskets. Most of the patterns had a medallion focus. Post-War newspaper articles confirm VFW and American Legion ladies' auxiliaries chose Poppy quilts for fund raising and also to honor the service of World War I veterans. Unfortunately, without stronger provenance, it is hard to estimate just how many Poppy quilts were made with this purpose in mind.

In Flanders Field
Written by Lieutenant Colonel John McCrae, a Canadian physician, May 3, 1915, after the death of a fellow soldier.

In Flanders fields the poppies blow
Between the crosses, row on row
That mark our place; and in the sky
The larks, still bravely signing, fly
Scarce heard amid the guns below.
We are the Dead. Short days ago
We lived, felt dawn, saw sunset glow,
Loved and were loved, and now we lie
In Flanders fields.
Take up our quarrel with the foe:
To you from failing hands we throw
The torch; be yours to hold it high.
If ye break faith with us who die
We shall not sleep, though poppies grow
In Flanders field.[26]

Evening Tribune
San Diego, California
October 10, 1928, page 9
WAR Mothers
To Make Quilts

Golden Poppy chapter. American War Mothers, will meet Friday, Oct. 12, in the American Legion rooms from 10 to 12 o'clock for sewing. "Mothers come, as we have four quilts to finish and other work to be done before the end of this year." It is requested.

Poppy Quilt made by Eula Mae (Weigle) Hiland (1895–1984), Cedar Rapids, Iowa and Ames, Iowa. 90 inches x 76 inches, cotton. Eula made the Poppy Quilt for her husband, John Erwin Hiland Sr. (1896–1987), who served his country and saw fighting on the battlefront in France. The young lieutenant's wife recalled, "My husband was in Flanders. He came home and told me how beautiful the poppies were, so I made him this quilt." Eula used a kit to make her memorable quilt.

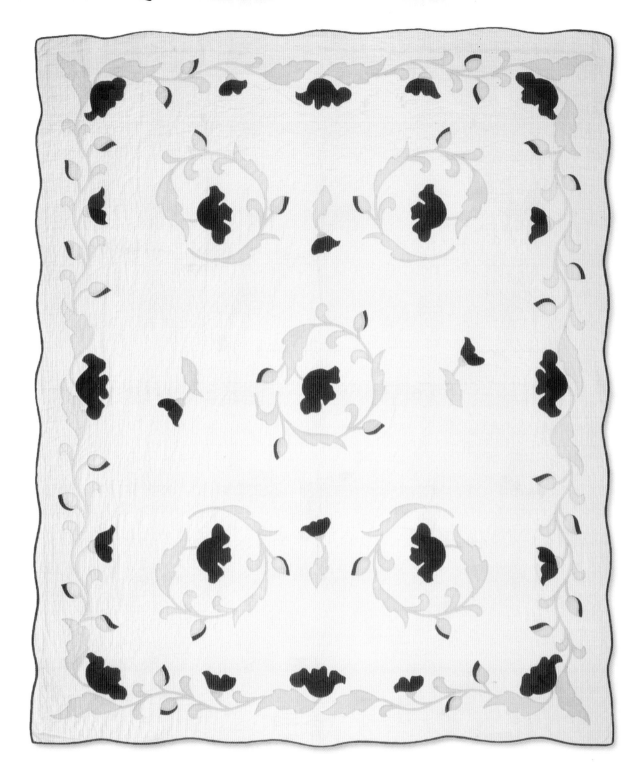

Wreath of Poppies Quilt, c. 1930, 75 inches x 91 inches, cotton. Courtesy of Mary Kerr.

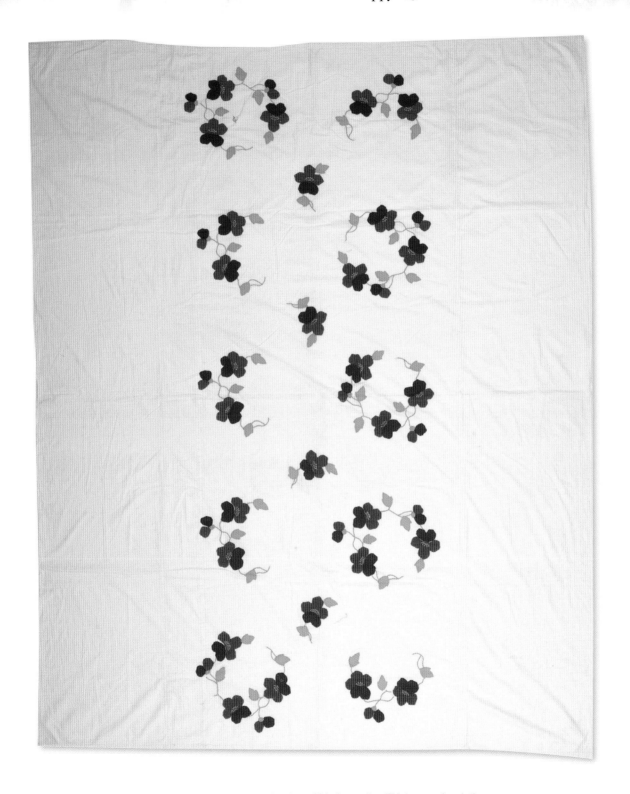

Wreath of Poppies Quilt, c. 1930, 76 inches x 90 inches, cotton. This top was done in the
same wreath design as the previous quilt, but with a different set.

Jefferson City Post Tribune
Jefferson City, Missouri
June 27, 1932, page 3

During the meeting the encampment (of the Veterans of Foreign Wars) presented a flag to the Sighted and Sightless Progressive Club of Springfield. Of interest also is the fact that the poppy quilt, which was made by Mrs. Tanner and donated to the encampment, was won by Mrs. R.J. McLain of St. Joseph. The proceeds from this quilt will go toward the building of a Missouri cottage at the national home of Veterans of Foreign Wars located at Eaton Rapids, Mich. For widows and orphans of over-seas men.

Register-Republic
Rockford, Illinois
May 17, 1937, page 8
Legion Auxiliary
Completes Plans
For Poppy Sale

Poppy day will be observed in Rockford this year on Saturday, May 22, Mrs. Arvid W. Anderson chairman of the poppy committee of American Legion auxiliary, has announced. Extensive preparations for the observance of the day are being made by the auxiliary women. Memorial poppies, to be worn in honor of the world war dead, and to raise funds for the welfare of the disabled veterans and needy families of the dead and disabled, will be distributed throughout the city.

The North Adams Transcript
North Adams, Massachusetts
July 14, 1939, page 14
Legion Auxiliary Notes

The regular meeting of Nelson E. Pickwell unit, No 15, American Legion Auxiliary was recently held at G.A.R. hall. The Poppy quilt given by Mrs. Agnes Plumb will soon be displayed in Medbury's window, and the sale of 10-cent articles, has already begun. All those members who have not handed in their 10 articles for the sale were urged to do so before July 15th. More boxes of greeting cards are being

Poppy Wreath, Kit designed by Progress No. 1349.
c. 1940, 81 inches x 99 inches, cotton.

Flanders Poppy, published
in the *Syracuse Herald,*
Syracuse, New York, April
3, 1934, page 24. Quilt
Book No. 21. This pattern
was another example of
what a post–World War I
Poppy quilt could look like.

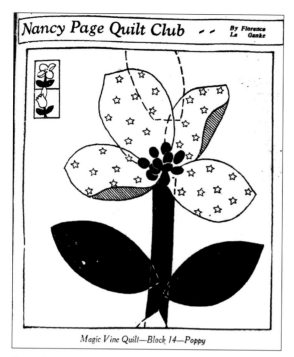

Nancy Page Magic Vine Quilt Club – Block 14 – Poppy. *Evansville Courier and Press,* Evansville, Indiana, April 19, 1931, page 25.

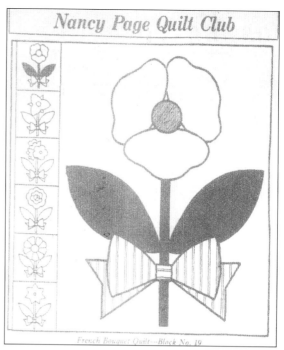

Nancy Page Quilt Club French Bouquet – Block 19 – Poppy. *Dallas Morning News,* Dallas, Texas, February 18, 1934, page 9.

ordered and orders for some are being taken by the members. Mrs. Mary Maynard was made chairman of a unique money making project for August which will be announced to the public later.

Mason City Globe-Gazette
Mason City, Iowa
November 6, 1940, page 12
Britt Legion
Group Meets.
Plans for a Pot Luck
Supper With Legion
On Nov. 11 Are Made
    BRITT—The American Legion Auxiliary met Monday night at its room in Liberty Memorial hall for their regular meeting. Plans were made for a joint pot luck supper with the Legion members on Armistice night, Nov. 11.
    Nov. 21, the Auxiliary will sponsor a carnival supper card game and a dance. A poppy quilt will be given away at 10 p.m. Nov. 21.

Mason City Globe-Gazette
Mason City, Iowa
March 20, 1941, page 24
Legion Auxiliary in
Corwith Has Session
    CORWITH—The American Legion Auxiliary of Elmer Wilson post No. 229 met at the home of Mrs. Lester Willrite southeast of Corwith Tuesday for an all day meeting.
    Mrs. Perr DeGroote, vice president presided at a business meeting following a pot luck dinner at noon. Members spent the day working on a "Poppy" quilt.

The Post-Register
Idaho Falls, Idaho
November 10, 1953, page 5
Rexburg Party Planned
(Special to The Post-Register)
    REXBURG, Nov. 10.—Rexburg Veterans of Foreign Wars Auxiliary have made plans to sponsor a luncheon and a series of card parties Nov. 20 to raise funds for the VFW Children's Home, VFW

Red, White and Blue Poppy Quilt, c. 1940, 73 inches x 92 inches, cotton. Most Poppy quilts are made in red and green.
This patriotic red, white and blue version was possibly made to honor a World War I veteran.

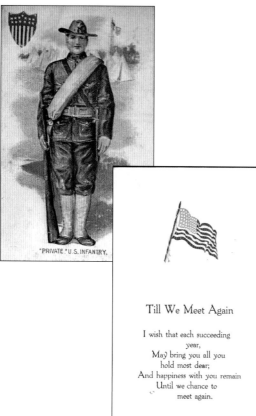

Till We Meet Again

I wish that each succeeding
year,
May bring you all you
hold most dear;
And happiness with you remain
Until we chance to
meet again.

Old Folks, and Veterans' Hospital in the lounge at the Veteran Memorial Hall. Mrs. Wilma Bean is in charge of the affair. There will be pinochle and bridge in play and the public is invited. Admission will be charged and the VFW poppy quilt will be on display.

When the Boys Come Home
by John Hay

There's a Happy time coming,
When the boys come home,
There's a glorious day coming
When the boys come home.
We will end the dreadful story
Of this treason dark and gory
In a sunburst of glory,
When the boys come home.

The day will seem brighter
When the boys come home,
For our hearts will be lighter
When the boys come home.
Wives and sweethearts will press them
In their arms and caress them,
When the boys come home.

The thinned ranks will be proudest
When the boys come home,
And their cheer will ring the loudest
When the boys come home.
The full ranks will be shattered,
And the bright arms will be battered
And the battle-standards tattered
When the boys come home.

Their bayonets may be rusty
When the boys come home,
And their uniforms dusty,
When the boys come home.
But all shall see the traces
Of battle's royal graces,
In the brown and bearded faces,
When the boys come home.

Our love shall go to meet them,
When the boys come home,
To bless them and to greet them,
When the boys come home;
And the fame of their endeavor
Time and change shall not dissever
From the nation's heart forever,
When the boys come home.[27]

NOTES

Silk American Flag, hand quilted with outline, cable and wave designs. This quilt belonged to General John J. Pershing, commander of American Expeditionary Forces in Europe during World War I. It was presented to the Nebraska State Historical Society by General Pershing's son, Warren Pershing. Courtesy of The Nebraska State Historical Society, Lincoln, Nebraska (O 7701-11).

1. http://en.wikipedia.org/wiki/American_Printing_Company_(Fall_River_Iron_Works)
2. *The Charleroi Mail*, Charleroi, Pa., October 1, 1910, page 3.
3. 1910 newspaper articles, unattributed (possibly the *Bridgeport Telegram*), provided by the Curtis family.
4. 1910 newspaper list of winners provided by the Curtis family, owners of the quilt.
5. *The Washington Post*, September 29, 1918, page 16.
6. "Historical Estimates of World Population" retrieved 29 March 2013.
7. *The Fort Wayne News and Sentinel*, "At the Sign of the Red Cross." October 3, 1918, page 8.
8. *The Washington Post*, "Flu Kills More Than War." November 18, 1918, page 7.
9. *The Fort Wayne News and Sentinel*, October 28, 1918, page 2.
10. *The Bedford Gazette*, Bedford, Pa., "Spanish Influenza." October 11, 1918, page 1.
11. *Daily Illinois State Journal*, Springfield, Ill., "Dr. St. Clair Drake Warns People to Use Care to Stop Pneumonia Spread." December 2, 1918, page 2.
12. *The Indianapolis Star Magazine*, "How Cupid Was Changed to Kewpie." April 5, 1915, page 63.
13. *Colorado Springs Gazette*, "Rose O'Neill." September 28, 1913, page 40.
14. Ibid.
15. Ibid.
16. *The Indianapolis Star Magazine*, "Rose O'Neil's Kewpies." September 10, 1913, page 40.
17. *Colorado Springs Gazette*, "Rose O'Neill." September 28, 1913, page 40.
18. Ibid.
19. *The Washington Post*, "More Kewpie Dolls." Washington, D.C., July 2, 1913, page 7.
20. *Hamilton Daily News Journal*, Hamilton, Ohio, "Interesting Facts." November 22, 1971, page 19.
21. *Bisbee Daily Review*, Bisbee, Ariz., "Man Enters Mountain Retreat of Mother of Kewpies." September 4, 1921, page 7.
22. 1918 Connecticut Red Cross Report.
23. www.greatwar.co.uk./people/moina-belle-michael.htm
24. *Greensboro Daily News*, Greensboro, N.C., "Poppy Day Will Be Observed Tomorrow." May 27, 1927, page 7.
25. www1.va.gov/opa/publications/celebrate/flower.pdf
26. www.usmemorialday.org/popup/flanders.htm
27. *Colorado Springs Gazette*, "Poems Old and New." February 3, 1918, page 12.

INDEX